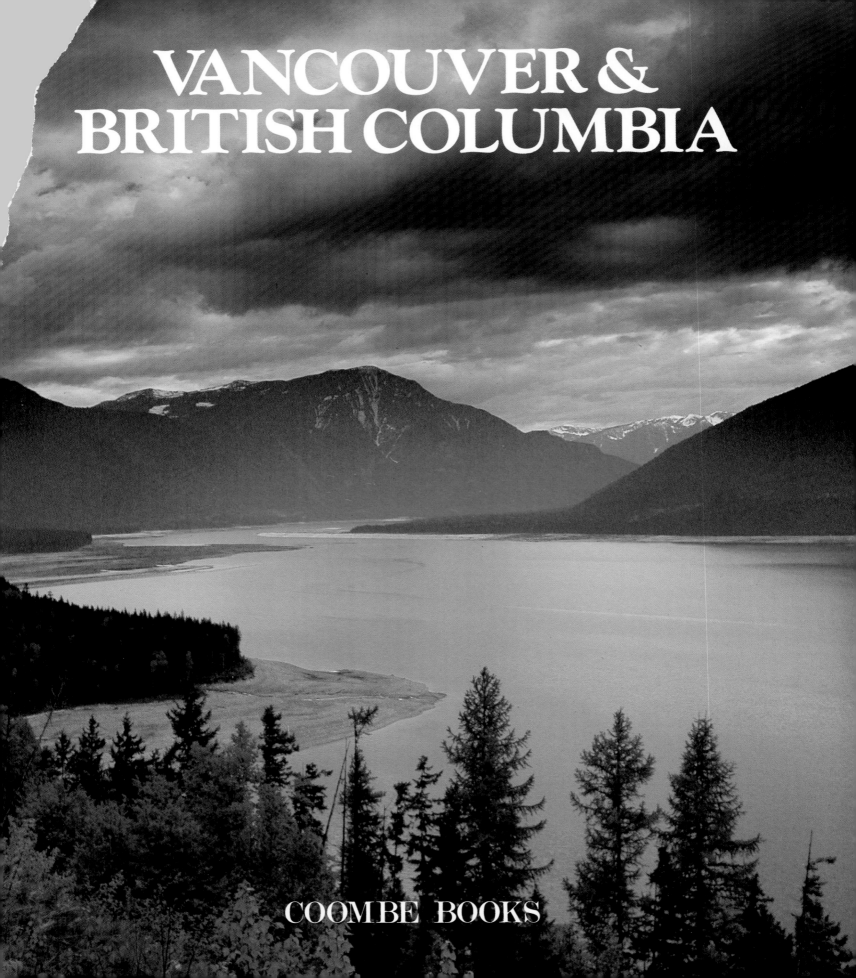

VANCOUVER &
BRITISH COLUMBIA

COOMBE BOOKS

CLB 1838
© 1987 Illustrations and text: Colour Library Books Ltd,
Godalming, Surrey, England.
This edition published in 1989 by Coombe Books.
Printed and bound in Hong Kong.
All rights reserved.
ISBN 0 86283 511 9

Splendor Sine Occasu – Splendour without Diminishment – British Columbia's motto describes this beautiful province perfectly. Stretching from the rugged Continental Divide to the waters of the Pacific, B.C. is Canada's third-largest province, trailing only Quebec and Ontario. At 948600km² (366,255 sq. miles), B.C. is bigger than France and Britain put together. It's big enough to contain comfortably California, Washington and Oregon. Vancouver Island, the site of Victoria, the province's gracious (and oh-so-British) capital, is somewhat larger than Belgium. Canada's gateway to the trading riches of the Orient and the Pacific Rim, B.C. is bounded to the north by the Yukon Territory along the sixtieth parallel; to the south by the U.S. border along the forty-ninth parallel and down the middle of Georgia Strait, Haro Strait and the

Facing page: Petersberg, one of the largest settlements along the coast north of Vancouver. Below: a ship on the Inside Passage.

Strait of Juan de Fuca; to the east by the province of Alberta, including a section of the Rocky Mountain Continental Divide, and to the west by the Pacific Ocean and the Alaska Panhandle.

Super, natural B.C. is a land of breathtaking excesses. The province is, as 19th century Liberal leader Edward Blake so nervously observed, "a sea of mountains." And indeed those indomitable ranges the Selkirk and the Monashee, the Cascades and the Coast Mountains do march protectively in parallel, giant steps across the province from the Divide to the Pacific. These mighty, snowcapped sentinels stand guard over nature's gifts to B.C.

And what an Eden this land is, with its surging rivers, its towering gorges and its lush, verdant valleys. B.C is a land of extremes, a land of blinding snowstorms and sensual sunsets, sparkling rainbows and secretive rain forests that surely belong in the Deep South rather than the True North. And it's big yellow suns shining brightly on the dry interior

plains; sparkling, lazy beaches and racing breakers pounding on the Pacific Shore. Above all, it's great stands of timber. Covering about 55 percent of the province, these great forests stretch in brooding majesty to eternity.

In a country amply endowed with more than its share of natural marvels, B.C. leads the way in the height of its mountains – many peaks of the St. Elias Range tower over 5200m; the force of its rivers – the turbulent, raging Fraser's Hell's Gate reduces even the most intrepid river travellers to awestruck silence; and the size and girth of its splendid trees. Little wonder that B.C has around 40 percent of Canada's marketable wood when the province is home to imposing red cedars and ancient Douglas Firs, some easily over 90m high, with trunks up to 4m in diameter!

A Canadian journalist once remarked that "British Columbians like to think of their province as a large body of land entirely surrounded by envy." Now whether

all Canadians envy British Columbians their lotus land all the time is a moot point: but certainly even the most loyal Easterners and Prairie dwellers will acknowledge that in February or March, B.C. is the place they'd rather be. For B.C.'s major population centres are blessed with Canada's mildest climate, and when the rest of Canada is still digging out from yet one more mid-winter snowstorm, residents of Victoria and Vancouver, the province's major cities, are admiring their host of golden daffodils.

Of course, in a province as large as B.C., climate is as varied as the people who live here. The three main factors that contribute to B.C.'s climate are the Pacific Ocean, the mountains and the province's northern latitude – B.C. stretches 11 degrees toward the Arctic. Coastal winters are kept mild and the summers cool thanks to the great Pacific Ocean stream called the Kuroshio (Japan) Current. The ocean also warms and saturates the prevailing easterly winds which roll over it and on to the shore. Here the Coast Mountains force the moisture vapour in the winds up into cooler air. This moisture vapour condenses and falls as rain or snow, depending on the time of year and the elevation. The west coast of Vancouver Island and the neighbouring Queen Charlotte Islands are the recipients of much of this moisture, making this one of the wettest spots on earth. It is this abundant rainfall, however, that is responsible for the region's splendid stands of red cedar, hemlock, Douglas fir and spruce.

Rain also falls freely on the mainland, but the amount varies with elevation and whether the mountain slopes face east or west. High mountains can receive more than 350cm of precipitation a year – mostly as snow. On the other hand, the lowlands and islands of the southern Strait of Georgia, which separates Vancouver Island from the mainland, generally receive less than 100cm of precipitation a year.

From the crest of the Coast Mountains, the Pacific wind rolls east into the interior plateau, up and over the interior ranges and down into the Rocky Mountain Trench. The up and over part of this roller coaster ride is usually wet; the down usually dry. The reason for this is quite simple:

the higher the hills, the more rainfall they can draw from the winds. This means that the immense Columbia Mountains average about 250cm of rain and snow a year. As a result, the vegetation on their western slopes is remarkably similar to that of the Coast Mountains. In the southern valleys of the interior, where the wind bottoms out, precipitation is less than 40cm a year, especially in the deep trenches of the Okanagan, Fraser and Thompson rivers. In some valleys, desert conditions prevail, for as little as 25cm of rain falls each year.

In the northern part of the interior, increasing latitude translates into longer, more severe winters. Occasionally, this part of the province feels the grip of a sub-zero deep freeze as intensely cold, clear air sweeps down from the Arctic.

Given that much of B.C. consists of mountains and forests and that the most hospitable climes exist in the southern quarter of the province, it's not surprising that most of B.C.'s 2.7 million residents live around the balmy lowlands of the Strait of Georgia.

Although B.C. was the last link in the European chain of settlement that established the foundations of modern Canada, it was here that the ancestors of the first Canadians – the Inuit and the North American Indians – arrived after their trek across the long-vanished land bridge of Beringia.

The earliest known B.C. sites of human habitation seem to date from about 12,000 years ago. Around this time the icefields of the last great glacial era began to retreat, enabling some of these long-ago hunters and fishermen to make their hesitant way inland.

In time, these wanderers coalesced into distinct peoples – the Haida, Kwakiutl, Tsimshian, Bella Coola, Nootka, Salish – with distinct territories of their own. By the late 18th century there were about 80,000 people living on the B.C. coast.

In general historical terms, settlement in B.C. is a fairly recent phenomenon. In Canadian terms, the province is geographically but an infant. Compared to the ancient rocks

Right: the majestic Queen of the North leaving Vancouver.

of the Pre-Cambrian Shield that cover much of the rest of Canada, B.C.'s mountains are real newcomers. The result of the earth's upheavals of the late Mesozoic Age, they date from a period less than 190 million years ago. And while it's doubtful that a volcanic eruption similar to neigh bouring Washington state's Mount St. Helens will occur in B.C., earthquakes are always a possibility, signifying perhaps that the earth's mountain-forming activities are not yet over in this part of the country.

But the force likely to have greatest impact on B.C. is not nature but people. For all its overwhelming magnificence and its plentiful natural resources – both renewable and non-renewable (timber, fish, minerals, fossil fuels and hydro power) – there's a fundamental vulnerability about B.C. that's well within human power to destroy.

The Indian inhabitants of B.C. lived in harmony with the land. Drawing on the salmon-filled rivers and the game-rich woods, they built their vibrant societies of plenty. When Captain James Cook sailed into Nootka Sound on March 29, 1778, becoming the first white man to land on what is now British Columbia territory, he noted the prosperity and rich ceremonial traditions of the Coast Indians. They lived in great houses of split cedar plants supported by elaborately carved posts. Their boats were beautifully decorated, as were their baskets, eating implements and other artifacts.

Although the area they inhabited was vast and their numbers comparitively small, there were apparently no less than eight different and quite distinct linguistic groups among the Indians. And within these groups there were again separate, distinct languages. But what struck Cook most was the Coast Indians' extraordinary sense of property. Wrote Cook, "I have no where in my several voyages met with any uncivilized

Previous pages: (left) Vancouver's west coast under sea fog, and (right) snow-capped peaks north of Squamish. Above: sunset at Long Beach and (facing page) a dense forest, both in Pacific Rim National Park.

nation, or tribe, who had such strict notions of their having a right to the exclusive property of everything that their country produces, as the inhabitants of this Sound."

Although he was the first European to set foot in British Columbia, Captain Cook was not the first to sight B.C. This honour goes to Sir Francis Drake. Sailing in the *Golden Hind*, he sighted the northwest coast in 1579, and claimed the misty shoreline for Queen Elizabeth I. Drake did not land in New Albion, as he called his find, nor did he enter the channel that the Greek Apostolos Valerianos, or Juan de Fuca as he is more commonly known, found in 1592. De Fuca mistook the

strait that now bears his name for the mythical Strait of Ainam, that marvellous inland sea believed to link the Atlantic to the Pacific.

B.C. was to remain a mystery to Europeans for almost another two centuries. So fanciful and unknown was this land that in 1726 Jonathan Swift placed Brobdingnag, his land of the giants in *Gulliver's Travels*, in the vicinity of the Queen Charlotte Islands. Perhaps Dean Swift's imaginings were not so far off target, because even today the nearby coastal mountains are home to Indian legends that tell of a race of giants called the Sasquatch.

Myth began slowly to make way for fact with the explorations of Vitus Bering. This intrepid Dane, voyaging eastward from Siberia for the Tsar of the Russias, had already explored much of Alaska before he died there of scurvy in the summer of 1741.

Less than thirty years later, in 1744, the Spaniard Juan Pérez, exploring northward from Mexico, sighted the Queen Charlotte Islands. Although he anchored off Vancouver Island and traded for furs with the Haida and Nootka Indians, he did not land there. Nor did Bruno de Hezeta and Juan Francisco de la Bodega y Quadra, who in 1775 also came northward to these waters.

Captain Cook and the crews of his ships, *Discovery* and *Resolution*, also traded for furs with the Indians. Of equal importance were the excellent relations Cook established with the Nootka chief, Maquinna, who greeted him wearing alternating masks and his bearskin whale-hunter's robe. So hospitable were the Indians that Cook named his anchorage Friendly Cove.

After Cook's death in Hawaii the following year, the *Resolution* and the *Discovery* sailed home via Whampoa, offloading the fine sea-otter pelts they had acquired from the Nootka to Chinese merchants for a handsome sum. When English merchants learned the high value of these furs at the court of the Chinese emperor, they lost little time outfitting further vessels to trade up and down B.C.'s coastal waters.

Right: a fishing boat amid the Broken Group Islands and (facing page) driftwood on South Beach, in Pacific Rim National Park.

The Spanish became indignant at this British intrusion into a region they laid claim to by right of prior discovery. Matters came to a head in 1789, when Estevan José Martinez arrived with a small flotilla to assert Spain's claims and promptly came face to face with Captain John Meares. Meares has earned his place

Below: an aerial view across Bute Inlet, the head of which offers fine views of Mount Waddington (facing page). Overleaf: (left) the Skeena River, in eastern British Columbia, and (right) Muncho Lake on the Alaska Highway.

in B.C. history for being the first European to acquire land in Canada west of the Rockies. He claimed that the land had been granted to him by Chief Maquinna. It probably had been, but whether the chief had any concept of European ideas of property ownership is highly doubtful. Meare's other great claim to fame is as the builder of the *North West America*, the first non-Indian-built craft to be launched on the coast.

Captain Meares promptly took his grievances to the British House of Commons. War between Spain and England was only avoided when Spain finally acceded to the old

principal that possession is nine-tenths of the law. The British had, after all, actually set foot on Vancouver Island, while the more timid Spanish had merely sailed along the coast. Under the terms of the Nootka Sound Convention, Spain returned Meares' land and compensated him for its seizure.

It fell to Captain George Vancouver, who had been a young officer on Cook's voyage, to implement the convention and further chart the coastline. In April 1792, Captain Vancouver arrived on the coast with the *Chatham* and the *Discovery*. Vancouver and his

Spanish counterpart, Commander Francisco de la Bodega y Quadra, got on particularly well. Together they circumnavigated and charted Vancouver Island – which Vancouver gallantly called Quadra and Vancouver Island – (Quadra was eventually dropped from the maps) and established that the Strait of Juan de Fuca did not lead to a great inland waterway or to the Northwest Passage. By the time Vancouver returned to England in 1794, he had sailed some 16,000km of B.C. coast.

But as is so typical of Canadian history, the fur trade was also to play a dominant part in developing B.C. On July 22, 1793, a young Scottish fur trader by the name of Alexander Mackenzie inscribed this message in grease and pigment on a rock at the mouth of the Bella Coola River: "Alex Mackenzie, from Canada, by land, 22nd July 1793." With these words Mackenzie established his rightful claim to being the first European to cross the American continent north of Mexico. Other fur traders, men of the Montreal-based North West Company, soon followed in Mackenzie's footsteps. In 1804, Simon Fraser established Fort McLeod, B.C.'s oldest surviving inland settlement. Fort St. James followed in 1806. It was at this latter site that a Vermont trader, Daniel Williams Harmon, started the first B.C. farm. Harmon raised potatoes, turnips, carrots and barley to supplement the dried salmon diet which the men at the fort had been living on.

The insatiable demands of the fur trade meant a continued quest for new fur-bearing areas. This spurred on exploration west of the Rockies. In 1808 Simon Fraser made his brave descent down the turbulent Fraser River en route to the Pacific. Fraser made the last leg of his journey in dugouts he and his party had bartered for with the indigenous Indians near Lillooet, in the lower Fraser Valley. Poor Fraser! When his journey came to an end at Point Grey, near the site of present-day Vancouver, he realized he had not been following the Columbia River as he had thought. Moreover, the river he had traversed at such peril

Left: the annual Prince George Professional Rodeo.

was certainly not suitable as a supply and transport route for the canoes of the fur trade. Little did he know, however, that seventy-five years later the Canadian Pacific Railway would follow this mighty river canyon to the Pacific, in the process unifying Canada from sea to sea – *A Mari usque ad Mare.*

In 1811, another Nor'Wester, David Thompson, was successful in surveying the Columbia River. But although the Nor'Westers liked to regard the whole of the Pacific Coast from Spanish California to Russian Alaska as their rightful domain, the restless Americans to the South thought otherwise. Lewis and Clark's famous expedition of 1803 had brought the explorers all the way from the Mississippi River to the mouth of the Columbia. This had led John Jacob Astor to envisage a string of fur forts – all flying the American flag – from the Rockies to the Pacific.

So when Thompson came to the mouth of the Columbia he was greeted by the stars and stripes fluttering in the breeze over Fort Astor. The fort was not destined to remain American for long, however. It became a casualty of the War of 1812, when it fell into the hands of the North West Company.

War in North America was not limited just to the British and the Americans. The great fur companies – the Hudson's Bay Company and the North West Company – competed hotly for control of the riches of British North America. Initially, the Hudson's Bay Company had exclusive trading rights east from the Continental Divide to the Great Lakes, while the Nor'Westers looked upon New Caledonia – as they called all the lands west of the Rockies to the Pacific – as their territory.

The one positive result of this ongoing competition between the two fur-trading companies was that by quite early in the 19th century all the major Canadian rivers east and west of the Great Divide had been traversed to their sources, and forts had been established all the way to the west coast.

In 1821, the North West Company was on the verge of bankruptcy and became amalgamated with the Hudson's Bay Company. The next twenty years saw the establishment of HBC posts all along the coast as the company attempted to hold off the restless Americans to the south and the Russians in Alaska to the north.

Initially, the headquarters of the HBC was Fort Vancouver. Built in 1825, the fort was near modern Portland in the Oregon Territory. But with growing American settlement and the expansionist mood of President Polk's administration, the Bay's days in Oregon Territory – the present states of Washington and Oregon – were numbered. "Fifty four Forty or Fight" was the cry for an American move northward – 54° 40′ being the southernmost border of Alaska.

Under the terms of the Oregon boundary treaty concluded in 1846 between Britain and the U.S., the 49th Parallel became the new frontier. A slight diversion at the western end gave the British southern Vancouver Island. The HBC moved its headquarters to the island, to the former Fort Camosun, now renamed Fort Victoria.

In 1849 Britain made Vancouver Island a Crown Colony, with the HBC's Fort Victoria as the main centre. James Douglas, the senior officer of the company, was also the island's administrator. After all, in that distant outpost of the empire, what benefited the HBC also benefited Her Majesty Queen Victoria.

Under the terms granting the Hudson's Bay Company exclusive trading rights in the territory, the company was required to promote settlement. And although settlement grew slowly, it did take root. The Puget Sound Agricultural Company, a subsidiary of the HBC, promoted the establishment of small farming communities in the southern part of the Island.

B.C.'s lumber industry began in 1848, the year the first sawmill was built at Victoria. The following year, the mill began to export lumber to San Francisco, beginning a pattern of north-south lumber trade dependency that continues to this day. (Nobody feels a decline in U.S. housing starts quicker than the workers in B.C.'s lumber industry!)

After coal was discovered in the northern part of the island, miners were brought over from England to work the seams at Fort Rupert and, five years later, in 1854, at Colville Town, present-day Nanaimo.

The island's first schoolhouse opened its doors in 1851. Democracy, of sorts, was established in 1856 with the holding of elections for the Legislative Assembly. This last development did not altogether please the autocratic Douglas. Up to this point he had ruled his vast domain and its less than 1000 white residents himself, assisted by a three-man Executive Council and an appointed Legislative Council made up primarily of HBC men, some of whom were related to him by marriage.

The push for democratization came from the British colonial

Cottonwood House (below) near Quesnel is one of the last remaining roadhouses along the scenic Cariboo Wagon Road, which leads to Barkerville (facing page), a restored gold-rush town.

secretary in answer to mounting criticism of the HBC's stranglehold on the Pacific Coast. Unfortunately, the qualifications for franchise were rather steep – freehold property to the value of £300. As a result, only forty people were eligible to vote in the island's first election. Democracy was seen to be done only in Victoria; elsewhere candidates to the assembly were nominated without opposition. Although the assembly-men were either current or past HBC employees, they were' not all ardent fans of Governor Douglas. And the assembly's speaker, Dr. John Sebastian Helmcken, the governor's son-in-law, proved himself also a man firmly wedded to proper parlia-

mentary procedure.

The little assembly was rather powerless and practically penniless in its first years. While the all-powerful HBC was backed by its considerable trading revenues and its profits from land sales, the assembly had only its liquor licence revenues to fall back on. But it did its best to provide a legitmate critical forum for the company-dominated administration. In the end, it was gold, rather than democracy, that catapulted Victoria and B.C. into a new age.

On Sunday, April 25, 1858, as Victorians in their Sunday best chatted to each other after church, an American side-wheeler called the

Above: the CN Railway crossing the North Thompson River, and (facing page) Mount Robson, the highest peak in the Canadian Rockies.

Commodore moored in the harbour just below the fort. The *Commodore's* 450 passengers – just about the population of Victoria itself – were mostly miners. And they were looking for gold. In no time, Victoria turned into a bustling frontier town of over 6,000 people. The HBC saw its supremacy wane as newcomers, many from San Francisco, made their fortunes supplying the more than 25,000 men who surged through the town en route to the mainland and the Cariboo gold fields on the Thompson

River.

By 1866 there were hundreds of stores and more than 80 saloons in Victoria. The population, hitherto almost entirely British, became a cosmopolitan mix of Americans, Italians, Germans, French and Chinese. A contingent of American blacks also came north from California and formed B.C.'s first volunteer military force.

The *Victoria Gazette* and the *British Colonist* came into being during those exciting years. Both newspapers were highly critical of the power wielded by the HBC in the colony and agitated stridently for wider powers for the legislature. But Governor Douglas had other concerns besides the clamorings of the *Colonist's* editor Amor De Cosmos.

In an effort to prevent the lawlessness that had characterized the California gold rush of 1849, Douglas insisted that all miners take out a licence in Victoria before they crossed the Georgia Strait and headed upriver.

Even more pressing than his fear of anarchy, was his fear of an American annexation of the mainland, still known as New Caledonia. By law, Douglas's authority extended only to Vancouver Island and the Queen Charlotte Islands. The Colonial Office in faraway London shared Douglas's anxiety, made all the more real by the fact that so many of the newcomers were Americans. So Lord Lytton introduced legislation into the imperial parliament to create government on the mainland. On August 2, 1858, the mainland became part of a new Crown Colony to be called British Columbia. Queen Victoria herself chose the name for the new territory, which stretched from the Continental Divide to the coast. Her Majesty also appointed James Douglas governor of the new colony. In assuming his new post, Douglas had to give up his job as chief factor of the HBC.

Even the iron-willed Douglas needed help to maintain law and order on the mainland. He got it in the form of a detachment of Royal Engineers and an extra screw-frigate, the *Tribune*, to reinforce the naval squadron. Douglas's greatest asset in the law and order division came in the distinguished personage of Judge Mathew Baillie Begbie, "the hanging judge of the Cariboo." The judge, an English expatriate who arrived in B.C. in 1858 at the age of 39, was famous for dispensing justice from atop his horse, in tents, shacks or barns. For all his reputation, Begbie never hanged a man who hadn't been convicted by a jury. The worthy judge was not without his enemies. Once, after overhearing two men below his hotel window plotting to do him in, the judge took the law into his own hands, so to speak, by emptying the contents of his chamber pot over their heads!

The Royal Engineers, who were sometimes called upon to back up Begbie's less popular decisions, were also put to work on projects more in keeping with their skill and training. Governor Douglas had chosen Fort Langley on the lower Fraser River to be the site of the new territory's capital. However, Colonel Richard Clement Moody, in command of the Royal Engineers, decided that Fort Langley was not a good spot to defend in case of American attack. Moody chose a wooded site on the northern part of the Fraser, where he proceeded to clear the woods and lay out a new town called Queensborough. On July 20, 1859, New Westminster (Queen Victoria didn't fancy Queensborough) was proclaimed capital of the mainland colony.

From time to time Douglas crossed to the mainland from Victoria to oversee his domain. There was no legislation council or assembly, but in Judge Begbie and Colonel Moody, Douglas found he had just the admirable advisors and supporters he needed.

In 1863 Douglas was knighted for his services to the Crown. The following year the Douglas era in B.C. history came to an end with his retirement as governor of Vancouver Island and British Columbia.

Declining gold production led the British Government to unite the two colonies in 1866, thereby cutting back on administrative expenses. New Westminster continued to be the capital of the combined territory for a couple of years. Finally, agitation from government officials, who

Right: the Robson River and Mount Robson, in Mount Robson Provincial Park.

much preferred the civilized comforts of Victoria to New Westminster's rustic charms, resulted in a free vote being held to decide the location of the capital. Victoria won – 14 to 5 – and became B.C.'s capital in 1868.

As befitted a capital city, Victoria looked to its British antecedents to find the right tone of gracious circumspection and dignity so appropriate for a seat of government.

And even today, while Victoria is definitely a city of late-20th century comfort and self-confidence, it has retained a charming awareness of the pleasure adhering to life's timeless little rituals can bring. In a nation favouring civility over brashness, Victorians are pre-eminent in their civilized manners and ready respect for the rights of their neighbours.

Below: the mottled leaves of devil's club, which grows by the boardwalk of Mount Revelstoke's Giant Cedars Trail (facing page).

There's a stately charm about Victoria that has to be savoured to be appreciated. You feel it in the long, afternoon cricket matches Victorians like to watch, or in the unhurried delight they take in their leisurely afternoon teas. Connoisseurs of this English ritual should not overlook taking tea at the old vine-covered Empress Hotel. Afternoon tea at the Empress is a Victorian delight of delicate sandwiches and dainty cakes and perfectly brewed tea, complemented by the finest of fine bone china. Long the centre of Victoria's social life, the Empress was designed by Francis Rattenbury, architect of the Parliament Buildings, and hoasts commanding views of Victoria Harbour.

Without a doubt one of the best ways to see Victoria is by bicycle. Sights not to be missed include Dr. John Sebastian Helmcken's house on Belleville Street, which looks much the same as it did when the young doctor and his bride Cecilia (one of

Governor Douglas's daughters) set up housekeeping there in 1852. The house was built of timbers handhewn from logs which had been hauled by oxen up from the beach at James Bay, and grew, section by section, to keep pace with the doctor's growing family.

Dr. Helmcken, who had come to Canada as a ship's physician on a HBC trading vessel, was not only the speaker of the province's first legislative assembly, but also one of the architects of B.C.'s entry into the Canadian Confederation in 1871.

The family of Stipendary Magistrate and Assistant Gold Commissioner Peter O'Reilly lived not far from the Helmckens in Point Ellice House. This lovely old home still gazes out over the north shore of the island's inner harbour.

Coal built Craigdarroch Castle, the massive, five-storey turreted home of Vancouver Island coal baron Robert Dunsmuir. The fabulously wealthy Dunsmuir had begun his career in

coal as one of the English miners brought out by the Hudson's Bay Company to work in the fledgling coal industry at Port Rupert and Nanaimo. Once the site of Victoria's most elegant balls and receptions, Craigdarroch suffered the ignominy of being auctioned off for a dollar following the death of Dunsmuir's wife, Joan. Dunsmuir himself had died just as the great Scottish-style castle was completed in 1889.

Not to be overlooked is Emily Carr House. Situated at 207 Grosvenor Street, this handsome Mid-Victorian home was the birthplace of one of B.C.'s – and Canada's – greatest artists.

And then there are the Parliament Buildings, which were opened in February 1898. A marvel of neo-gothic architecture, the Parliament Buildings took four years to build for the grand sum of $923,000. The crowning glory of this wonderland of stained glass windows, marble panels, sweeping staircases, and intricate, inlaid mosaic-tiled floors is the copper-covered central dome topped with a golden statue of Captain Vancouver.

But there's more to Victoria than just buildings. Lying like verdant oases within the bricks and mortar of the city is a series of wonderful parks. With its mild winters and its balmy summers, Victoria is a gardener's delight, a fact fragrantly and picturesquely evident in the well-tended gardens that are the pride of most of Victoria's homeowners. This love of floral beauty carries over into the city's parks. Not to be missed are Crystal Gardens and Beacon Hill Park, long Victoria's favourite recreation spot. The park gets its name from the beaconfires that used to be lit here to warn mariners of a dangerous, submerged reef lying just offshore. Originally the site of pre-historic burial mounds, Beacon Hill was the first designated park in the province. In spring, Beacon Hill Park is a wondrous sea of yellow gold, as thousands upon thousands of

Right: a stream tumbles over rocks and boulders and (facing page) hikers admire Sugar Loaf Mountain in Glacier National Park.

daffodils bloom everywhere among the green grass. May brings tulips followed by glorious rhododendrons and the vibrant purples and magentas of masses of azaleas.

Picnicking on Beacon Hill, with the sunlight teasing the waters of nearby Juan de Fuca Strait, the lofty Olympic Mountains looming protectively across the waters in Washington State, and the giggles and squeals of the children feeding the swans and ducks in the ponds below, is enough to make anyone sell up everything and move to Victoria. (Incidentally, the city is a favourite retirement site for Canadians who, having once visited Victoria, fell in love with the place and determined to move here as soon as they could.) Mile 1 of the 4860 mile (7821km) Trans-Canada Highway, the longest national highway in the world, starts at Beacon Hill.

North of Victoria is the Saanich

Below: Asulkan Valley and (facing page) Dome Point and the Asulkan Glacier seen from Abbott Ridge, all in Glacier National Park.

Peninsula. Uncharacteristically for B.C., this is not a region of great mountains and fast-flowing rivers. It's a land of tranquil farms, dappled country lanes, sleepy old churches and quiet coastal beaches that invite you to dig for tasty littleneck and butter clams. "Saanich" comes from an Indian word meaning "fertile soil". The Saanich is berry territory – loganberries, boysenberries, strawberries and raspberries grow wonderfully here, with loganberries being the peninsula's major crop. Daffodils are also another important Saanich export: well over 13 million blooms a year are shipped out from Saanichton alone. But perhaps the Saanich Peninsula's most unique crop is Christmas holly, which every December finds its way into homes all across Canada.

The Saanich is also a birdwatcher's delight, but its star attraction, the English Slylark, is definitely easier to hear than to see. Introduced to the island by homesick English settlers, the buffy-brown little birds thrive in this peaceful world of hedges and violets and graceful Japanese cherry blossoms.

Not to be missed on a visit to the Saanich is Butchart Gardens, overlooking Tod Inlet near Brentwood Bay. This floral paradise, reclaimed from the maw of an old limestone quarry, consists of several distinctive sections. The Italian Garden, the Japanese Garden and the English Rose Garden are planned to bloom year round. Many of the plants were collected by the gardens' founders, Robert and Jenny Butchart, who began the gardens as a hobby in 1904. The gardens, which are approached along a road lined with 500 flowering cherry trees, should be visited both during the daytime and at night. Illuminated under a clear Saanich sky, they are an

Above and overleaf right: Mount Odaray Plateau Grand View in Yoho National Park (facing page), and (overleaf left) the township of Field, which lies at the heart of this beautiful park.

enchanting, magical place of sparkling ponds and glistening waterfalls and the bewitching fragrance of countless blooms.

Swartz Bay, on the northern tip of the Saanich Peninsula, is the jumping-off point for the lovely, unspoiled Gulf Islands. Scattered in the Strait of Georgia and sheltered by Vancouver Island, the Gulf Islands enjoy the mildest winter climate in Canada. They are the year-round home of many of Canada's writers, artists, potters, weavers and determined individualists.

The main islands are Saltspring, Mayne, North and South Pender,

Galiano, Saturna and Thetis. There are over 100 islands – one of which is said to have been owned by Elvis Presley – in the archipelago, which extends southward through the International Boundary. The American group is known as the San Juan Islands.

The first Europeans to come to these islands were the Spanish, in 1791. For centuries, however, they had been visited by the Nanaimo and Cowichan Indians from Vancouver Island, and the Salish, Musqueam and Tsawwassens from the southern mainland. Among the first settlers were a group of blacks – many of them former slaves – from California. They applied to James Douglas for permission to settle on Saltspring Island in 1857.

Because the soil-cover on the islands is comparatively thin, they

are not suited to extensive agriculture. Sheep do well on the islands, as the annual July 1st Saturna Lamb Barbecue so tastily attests. During the dry years of Prohibition, rumrunning from the little coves around Pender Island to Seattle was a favourite – and profitable – activity for Canadians and Americans alike. Today's islanders seem content to restrict their beach activities to finding succulent oysters, rock Dungeness crabs and clams.

Deer roam the islands, stopping occasionally to sample the produce in backyard gardens. Gulf Islanders seem to enjoy the best of both worlds – close enough to big city diversions and services when they want them, and yet happily removed from the relentless pace of the nine-to-five world.

What lamb is to Saltspring, the famous Cowichan sweaters are to the Cowichan Valley region of Vancouver Island, an easy drive from Victoria. Cowichan sweaters are made from naturally colored raw

wool. Heavy with original lanolin oil, they are rain-resistant and extremely durable. Their distinctive patterns are derived from those on cedar bark and mountain-goat wool blankets once worn by Coast Salish Indians. (Perhaps the most famous owners of Cowichan sweaters are Charles and Diana, the Prince and Princess of Wales, who received Cowichan sweaters as wedding presents.)

The Cowichan Valley is also dairying country. Herds of fine Holsteins graze in the fertile farms wrested by the settlers from the forests. Cowichan cows supply much of B.C.'s milk. Lumbering is still very important in this region, and motorists are required at all times to yield to the convoys of logging trucks that travel Cowichan's backroads.

Further up Vancouver Island's coast is Port Alberni, site of B.C.'s first sawmill for cutting timber for export. Most people think of Port Alberni as being just a logging community, because of its connection with the giant pulp and paper company,

MacMillan Bloedell. However, Port Alberni is also home to a large, modern fishing fleet of more than 300 vessels, whose yield accounts for over 20 percent of B.C.'s salmon catch.

But since the biggest trees in the world grow in the rain forests of the Pacific Coast, a visit to the region's MacMillan Provincial Park is a must. Here, in aptly named Cathedral Grove, you may rubberneck at giant Douglas firs, some more than 75m (240 feet) high. Some of these great trees were mere saplings when Cabot sailed to North America in 1497. Western red cedar, western hemlock, Sitka spruce and broadleaf maple trees also grow in the park.

On the west coast of the island is spectacular Pacific Rim National Park. This park, which covers approximately 150sq. miles, is divided into three quite distinct sections – Long Beach, the Broken Islands Group and the West Coast Trail. Long Beach is an 11-kilometre crescent of hard-packed, pale golden sand and endless breakers, skittish and playful, beckoning surfers and fishermen alike. But sunbathers who've basked on the Pacific shores, and lazily watched sea lions taking their ease on nearby rocks, know that the same Pacific can turn moody and petulant very quickly. At such times the ocean's an awesome sight as it whips itself into a crashing, seething frenzy that slams into the coast, while overhead thunder rolls and the skies dump a torrent of steaming rain.

Long Beach is the place to dream dreams of faraway places. Here, as the morning mists recede, the ever watchful beachcomber will likely stumble on a little glass fishing float in amongst the twisted, gnarled driftwood: a little souvenir from a fisherman's net in distant Japan, washed ashore by the mysterious night tides.

The Broken Islands Group in the mouth of Barkley Sound consists of ninety-eight scattered islands, rocks and reefs. Habour seals favour the islands' sheltered inlets, and Pacific gray whales can also be seen. Thousands of birds have their rookeries here, including pelagic cormorants, Canada's smallest, most marine species, and the powerful bald eagle.

The Broken Islands Group is a favourite with scuba divers. At least fifty ships have gone to their doom here in the "graveyard of the Pacific" over the last century.

The West Coast Trail, which begins at Pachena Bay, is an old lifesaving route for shipwrecked sailors. In 1890 a telegraph line had been installed along the trail to connect with lighthouses at Carmanah Point and Cape Beale. In this way news of shipwrecks could be relayed to Victoria. Small huts containing emergency supplies were located along the trail to provide succor to survivors. Modern rescue methods have made the trail obsolete, but it's still a fascinating

Facing page: Mount Harkin. Left: a coyote in Kootenay National Park. Overleaf: (left) Fort Steele Historic Park, a recreation of an 1890s Kootenay town, and (right) a sawmill by Slocan Lake, near Nelson.

route to hike, providing you know what you're doing and are not daunted by excessive damp. Above all, you must be able to judge the tides when the trail takes you along the wild seashore.

North-east of Pacific Rim, through the island's rugged interior, is Strathcona Provincial Park. B.C.'s oldest park covers 2310km² (about half a million acres) and was named after Donald Alexander Smith, First Baron Strathcona and Mount Royal, who is renowned for having driven in the famous last spike on the railway linking the Atlantic to the Pacific. Here roam the island's last herd of elk, as well as wolverine, coast deer, cougars and wolves. Western red

Facing page: the winding Bishop River, joined by myriad mountain streams, and (below) a lone rower on Pavilion Lake near Lillooet.

cedar and Douglas fir surround the lofty mountains that dominate the park. Of these mountains, the 2200-metre (7,219 feet) Golden Hinde, Vancouver Island's highest peak, thrusts majestically out of the wilderness of the park's centre. Strathcona park abounds in lakes, rivers and creeks, and its high slopes are covered in an endless, bright carpet of wildflowers. One of the world's highest waterfalls, Della Falls, is located in the southern section of the park. The great cascade of Della Falls plummets 440m over three spectacular chutes to Della Lake below.

Strathcona Park is the back door to Campbell River country, renowned for its fighting Chinook salmon. Up the coast from Campbell River, through some of the most peaceful, unspoiled terrain imaginable, is Port Hardy. Here you can take the *Queen*

of the North to Prince Rupert on the mainland. Tumbling waterfalls, magnificent mountains, glimpses of wildlife and fishing boats hauling in their catch are just some of the memorable sights the Inside Passage ferry journey has to offer. Definitely the most unforgettable sound of the Inland Passage boat trip is the *k'sss k'sss* of the killer whales and dolphins that love to follow the ferry. Watching these splendid creatures leap out of the water to bestow their affectionate kisses is definitely one of the great delights of Inland Passage travel.

From Prince Rupert you can reach the Queen Charlotte Islands by plane or ferry. Named for the wife of King George III, the 250km-long archipelago consists of about 150 islands. Two of these islands, Graham and Moresby, account for most of the islands' approximately 9000km².

These pages: the calm waters of Lillooet Lake, surrounded by magnificent, densely forested mountains.

There are some B.C. residents who assert that, the beauty of their province as a whole notwithstanding, the Queen Charlottes work a strange, unrivalled magic that overshadows B.C.'s other more conventional charms. Having said this, however, it's also fair to say that the islands are not to everyone's taste. The silent forests and stern mountains can seem oppressively bleak – almost malevolent. Roads are rough and electricity scarce, and the lumber camps, iron mines and crab canneries that provide islanders with work, offer very little in the way of scenic beauty. So what's the appeal of these, the most isolated islands in Canada? Quite simply, there's a primeval beauty in the wildness of the Charlottes that has to be experienced to be appreciated.

Archeology tells us that the islands have been inhabited for about 8000 years. The Queen Charlottes are the ancient home of the Haida Indians. The Spaniard, Juan Perez, was the first European to discover the islands, in 1774. When Captain Cook visited the Charlottes, in 1778, there were about 6000 Haida. Contact with the Europeans brought the inevitable decimating diseases. By 1915 there were only about 580 Haida left. Today there are about 1500.

Another near casualty was the sea otter. So highly prized were sea-otter pelts for the lucrative China trade that, just forty years after Captain George Dixon began trading with the Haida for these pelts, the sea-otter was almost extinct.

The Haidas were expert hunters and fishermen and fearless warriors, paddling their handsomely carved, great war canoes as far south as Washington state. Traditionally, all Haida are members of one of two clans – the Raven and the Eagle. Marriage partners have always been sought from the opposite clan, with clan membership being passed on from mother to child.

The importance of the clan was displayed through elaborate, inherited family crests, which were carved on giant totem poles. These great, sturdy cedar poles, which the Haida erected in front of their houses, could be over 1m in width at the base, rising up to a height of 15m.

Haida culture fared badly under the Europeans, especially the administrators and missionaries, who viewed Haida beliefs and ceremonies with suspicion and distaste. Particularly strange – and therefore most suspect – were their Potlatch ceremonies. Potlatches were celebrations of feasting, spirit dances and chanting, at which the host would give elaborate gifts to all the guests, who would reciprocate at a later date. Failure to do so meant instant social disgrace. Alarmed by this bewildering largesse, the Europeans banned potlatches in 1884. The ban was to remain in effect until 1951, with disastrous consequences for Haida art and culture.

Fortunately, potlach and other Haida customs are now enjoying a revival. Haida craftsmen like Robert Davidson, a master carver, print-maker, and jeweller, are once more at work and their marvellous carvings and artworks are highly prized by European, American and Canadian collectors.

The resurgence of Haida art and culture has contributed greatly to the Haida's present justified desire to redress many of the wrongs done them in the past. Unsettled land claims and a militant defence of the islands' forests against further incursions by the lumber industry are two major concerns of the Haida, concerns in which they enjoy the support of many British Columbians.

Ironically enough, the Haida – and the Queen Charlottes – never had a truer champion than a genteel daughter of Victoria, one Emily Carr (1871-1945). One of Canada's foremost painters, Carr made periodic trips to the Charlottes. Her vigorous, colorful canvases capture the untamed splendor of the whole west coast, and provide a haunting record of those vanished villages, houses and totem poles that reflected the past glory of the Haida. Carr was also a talented writer, and her collection of literary sketches *Klee Wyck* (Carr's Indian name, meaning "Laughing One") is a marvellous record of the effect of Northwest Coast Indian life on the artist herself.

UNESCO has also come to the rescue by declaring the old Haida village of Ninstints, on Skungwai Island, with its spectacular totem poles, a World Heritage Site.

When you return from the Queen Charlotte Islands to Prince Rupert, you can't help but feel that you have stepped from the past straight into

Below: ploughed land and (facing page) blossoming orchards in the beautiful Okanagan Valley, the "fruit basket of Canada".

the future. Prince Rupert, named for the first Hudson's Bay Company governor, is the industrial and commercial centre for northwest B.C. It's also the halibut capital of the world. Other important catches of its ultra-modern fishing fleet include salmon, lingcod, herring and sole.

The vast golden harvests of the prairies destined for export to the markets of the Pacific Rim are shipped from Prince Rupert. Built around a magnificent, natural, ice-free harbor, Prince Rupert is the most important port in B.C. after Vancouver.

Highway 16 from Prince Rupert follows first the Skeena and then the Bulkley rivers to Prince George. The muddy Skeena, as old-time British Columbians affectionately refer to the river, has a lively seal population whose antics always entertain travellers. Seals have not always been so popular: not that long ago they were looked upon as a real pest for their destructive fishing habits. It seems the seals would take just one bite from each salmon they caught rather than dining on the whole fish.

This wasteful practice led to the introduction of a bounty on seals. Hunters would go out in boats and shoot the seals, turning in their noses to collect the bounty.

The communities between the two Princes are as varied as the terrain itself. Port Edward's main industry is fishing; Terrace's is lumber; Kitimat, just south of the Skeena, on the Kitimat River, was once primarily an aluminum town. And although the Alcan smelter, the original reason for Kitimat's birth in the 1950s, is one of the worlds great metallurgical plants, Kitimat is renowned as a pulp-and-paper and logging centre and for its growing petrochemical concerns.

The Skeena River Valley is Gitksan Indian territory – "Skeena" is Gitksan for "river of mists." In addition to Indian communities in little towns along the Skeena like Kitwanga, there is a marvellous reconstruction of a Gitksan Indian village at the junction of the Skeena and Bulkley rivers at Hazleton. There have been Indian villages at this site for thousands of years. 'Ksan's cedar longhouses and elabo-

These pages: colour and excitement at the Molson World Downhill Championships at Whistler Ski Village.

rately carved totem poles, its fish traps, smokehouses and dugout canoes, look just as they did when the first whites arrived here in 1872. Past Hazleton, Highway 16 winds its way through Bulkley River country, definitely a must for serious anglers. Each fall, thousands of salmon make their way up the river to spawn, and intrepid fishermen will want to try spearing their supper, Indian style, from the rocks neat Morricetown. Fanciers of steelhead trout should head straight for the town of Telkwa, where some of the biggest steelheads in the world have been caught.

Not so long ago, the road through this beautiful land of mountains and valleys and lakes was a twisting, turning, winding gravel route that added miles – and hours – to the journey to Prince George. But not any more. In no time you're in Vanderhoof, the geographic centre of British Columbia. And then you

arrive at Prince George.

This booming metropolis of around 70,000 people is the major manufacturing, supply and government administration centre for northcentral British Columbia.

Prince George is also the gateway to the north. From Prince George the Hart Highway (Highway 97) leads northeast for about 400km to Dawson Creek, the southern terminus of the Alaska Highway and

the "capital" of B.C.'s Peace River Region. Alexander Mackenzie crossed the area in 1793 and Simon Fraser established North West Company trading posts along the Peace, Athabaska and Laird rivers, the main waterways of the region.

Dawson Creek is mile "0" on the Alaska Highway, that great Canadian-American road built in the dark days of World War II when Japanese invasion seemed imminent. The Alcan Military Highway, as it was then called, was built in eight months, dense forest wilderness and five mountain ranges notwithstanding. The highway, all 2451km, stretches all the way to Fairbanks, Alaska, and is almost as big a

challenge to maintain as it was to build. With winter temperatures dropping to −48°C, bulldozer blades have been known to crack like glass and become powerless to shift the snows that blizzards dump on the highway. Spring brings new problems in the form of floods and landslides.

Some of the world's richest farmlands are found in the foothills and plains of Peace River country. Rapeseed grows particularly well here, thanks to the rich soil and long, midsummer days. Nothing indicates the plenty and peace for which this region is so well named than fields of abundant, yellow, ripening rapeseed, sighing gently in the breeze under

Facing page: a mountain near Squamish, and (below and overleaf right) skiing centres in the snow-clad Rockies near Whistler Mountain. Overleaf left: Lake Garibaldi.

These pages: views of Vancouver, with the domed British Columbia Place Stadium in the foreground (facing page).

cloudless, bright blue skies.

In addition to its agricultural riches, the region also has coal and petroleum reserves and vast hydro-electric power capacity generated by the Peace River powerhouse, formed by the construction of the W.A.C. Bennett Dam near the town of Hudson Hope.

But if the Peace, Laird and Athahaska rivers mean life to B.C.'s north, the mighty Fraser is really the river of life for the whole province, for B.C. actually came into being around the fierce, fast-flowing Fraser. Rising at 54°55' north latitude, the Fraser begins its life innocently enough in two small streams fed by the glacier of towering Mount Robson in the Rocky Mountains.

The Fraser River is 1368km long, with a drainage basin of 238000km². For much of its length it's a savage, rebellious river determinedly warring with the maze of mountains and ridges that would subvert its efforts to flow to the Pacific.

The Fraser was named by the explorer David Thompson in honour of Simon Fraser, who had followed the river's course to its mouth in 1808. (Simon had already named the Thompson River in honour of David.) The son of a loyalist officer who had died in prison during the American Revolutionary War, Fraser had joined the North West Company as a clerk at the age of sixteen. By 1801 he was a partner in that great enterprise and in 1805 was put in charge of all the company's operations beyond the Rockies.

The diaries he has left us of his great journey down the Fraser still make for thrilling reading more than 170 years later. By June 19th, 1808, Fraser's party had reached the junction of the Fraser and Thompson rivers, just north of present-day Lytton. On June 20, the party set out on the most perilous part of the trip, traversing the steep Fraser Canyon.

Here, amidst towering cliffs, their canoes were carried along at frightful speeds by the remorseless pull of the Fraser's currents and spun dizzyingly in whirlpools and eddies until they were finally swept ashore.

"As for the journey by land," begins Fraser's diary entry for June 26, "we could scarcely make our way in some parts even with our guns. I have been for a long period among the Rocky Mountains, but have never seen anything equal to this country ... We had to pass where no human being should venture."

Less than half a century after Fraser's epic voyage, gold was to start a stampede of fortune-seekers up the river. Gold had been found first on the North Thompson in 1857. The Hudson's Bay Company had issued the local Indians with iron spoons to dig the scales out of cracks that had formed in the bedrock. Not long after, the bars of the Fraser were also found to contain gold. When the first consignment reached the assay office in San Francisco, word got out and the Cariboo gold rush was on.

Men – and some women – came from all over the world to mine the rich Cariboo ore. Gold fever drove them to risk their lives ascending the Fraser to pan the sand-bars at Hope

Above: downtown Vancouver, and (facing page) a view north over the city towards the Coast Mountains.

and Yale, Williams Lake and Quesnel, Barkerville and Soda Creek. Some made and spent vast fortunes; others toiled for little or no reward or eventually drifted away to seek their Eldorado elsewhere. Still others never even made it to the site of their dreams, but perished in the swirling waters of the Fraser, leaving their flimsy wooden rafts to bob drunkenly along the river for the rocks and rapids to claim.

Whatever else gold did, it certainly brought life to the B.C. mainland, for the prospectors became the nucleus of the mainland's population. Perhaps the most famous of the B.C. towns that gold built was Barkerville. Situated on Williams Creek, Barkerville was once the biggest community west of Chicago and north of San Francisco. At a time when Victoria had no more than 6,000 inhabitants, rip-roaring Barkerville had at least 10,000.

It was here on August 21, 1862, that a Cornish miner-cum-seaman by the name of Billy Barker struck the motherlode. Barker and his partners were to mine gold to the value of $600,000. The sprawling, muddy town named in Barker's honour boasted hotels, banks, laundries, barber shops, bakeries, blacksmiths and a number of lively ladies to divert the weary miners from their backbreaking labours. There was a library for the more literate, churches for those who could perceive the mortal dangers to their souls afforded by some of Barkerville's less reflective pursuits, touring theatre companies from San Francisco and even a twice-weekly newspaper, the *Cariboo Sentinel*.

Alas, poor Barkerville was wiped out by fire in 1868. The conflagration, which lasted no more than eighty minutes, is believed to have caused over $1 million worth of damage. Although Barkerville was hastily rebuilt, its days as a boom town were numbered. As the more accessible gold was worked out, only large, well-financed companies had the funds needed to exploit the riches of the deep shafts.

Today, the gold capital of the Cariboo has been restored to show off some of its former rowdy glory. The site is now a 65-hectare provincial historic park. Over 70 of the 1868-69 buildings have been reconstructed or restored. Visitors can enjoy a hearty meal of sourdough bread and stew at the "Wake-Up Jake" Coffee Saloon and Lunch House and watch the girls swish their skirts and lacy petticoats at the old Théâtre Royale.

Left: Canada Place, overlooking modern sculpture and restful greenery in Granville Square, Vancouver.

Poor Billy fared less well than his namesake. In 1863 Billy had married a widow from Victoria, a woman whose inherent good taste just needed money to nourish into full flower. Needless to say, as fast as Billy extracted gold from the ground, Mrs. Barker helped him spend it. Billy died penniless in an old men's home in Victoria on July 11, 1894, and was buried in a pauper's grave.

In addition to population, gold bought the mainland another impetus for development – the Cariboo Road. The road was Governor Douglas's idea. Douglas saw that such a road would benefit not only the miners, who had to pay as much as $300 for a barrel of flour, so difficult was it to transport supplies to the interior. More important to Douglas, the road would open up the interior to permanent settlement.

Without waiting for British government approval, Douglas borrowed £50,000 to finance his project. Work began in 1862, with the most difficult stretches of the road being laid by the colony's company of Royal Engineers. The bulk of the road was constructed by private contractors, including Mr. Joseph W. Trutch, who was to play an important role in shepherding B.C. into Confederation. Running some 650km along the Fraser River Canyon between Yale and Barkerville, the Cariboo Road was opened in 1864. Mule trains used to travel the route, bringing supplies to the mining camps. With dizzyingly sheer drops from the road's unguarded lip, man or beast need only stumble once to hurtle to instant death below. Even today, the Cariboo Highway is one of the most spectacular – and tricky – roads in North America.

Highway 20, west of Williams Lake, goes through Chilcotin country. Here tens of thousands of beef cattle, mostly Herefords, roam vast, unfenced grasslands. The 5000-square-kilometre plateau that makes up the Chilcotin lies between the Fraser River and the Coast Mountains. The Chilcotin has been mainly ranching country since settlement began here in the 1860s, with the hungry miners of the Cariboo gold fields being the first customers for Chilcotin beef.

The Chilcotin is regarded by many

cowboys as the last true Wild West. It's an unforgettable land immortalized by Paul St. Pierre in his great stories *Breaking Smith's Quarter Horse* and *Chilcotin Holiday* and celebrated annually in the high-spirited Anahim Lake Stampede, one of the few remaining authentic, old-style rodeos. Unlike many other rodeos across North America, Anahim is not reminiscent of a scene from "Dallas." It's a genuine get-together for ranchers and cowboys that enables the latter to show off their skills for the sheer pride of doing so and the former to rekindle old friendships and just socialize. Anahim means sociable campfires

Facing page: Granville Bridge, glimpsed through the masts of yachts moored in False Creek. Below: sunset over Burrard Inlet.

crackling in the still July night, guitars strumming, and beer flowing. And it's also talk of the good old days when the rancher was king in the Chilcotin, and didn't have to think about loggers and miners and tourists and government controls and regulations.

The Chilcotin is a land of rugged individualists, of whom the legendary Norman Lee is the rule rather than the exception. In 1898, Lee decided to drive a herd of 200 cattle from the Chilcotin to Dawson City in the Yukon, over 2400km (1,500 miles) away, where he knew the Klondike gold miners were always hungry for fresh beef. On May 17, Lee, the cattle, 30 horses, 5 cowboys, a horse wrangler and a cook set off. To make their tale of woe short, the horses contracted fever north of Hazelton and died, leaving

Lee and his men to continue on foot. As winter approached they decided to slaughter the cattle. The meat was loaded on scows, which were later lost on Teslin Lake in a storm, just 800km (500 miles) short of Dawson City. The penniless Lee made his way back to the Chilcotin, via Vancouver, having had to trade his winter coat to pay for passage on a coast boat for himself and his dog.

B.C.'s other great ranching territory is the Cariboo, that loosely defined region that comprises the area east of the Fraser's vast trench.

Of necessity, ranches in these parts are big. With the rangeland soil often thin, the terrain rocky and the rainfall low, small homesteads stand little chance of surviving. Of all the Cariboo cattle ranches, perhaps the most famous is that of the Douglas Lake Cattle Company in the south

Cariboo, which is owned by Charles (Chunky) Woodward, chairman of the Woodward's department store chain. In a country where water and good grass mean self-sufficient success, Douglas lake is blessed with both. Not surprisingly it's one of Canada's – and the world's – great cattle ranches.

Any journey through Cariboo Country takes you through towns like 150 Miles House, Lac La Hache, 100 Mile House, Clinton, Cache Creek and Lillooet, each with its own tale to tell of its role in opening up the B.C. interior. The drive between Lillooet and 150 Mile House is over part of the old Cariboo Waggon Road, B.C.'s oldest mainland road. Starting at Lilloet, every 25 miles or so a roadside station was built for the use of the roadgangs and later for travellers. The stations were called Mile Houses, hence the town names 25 Mile House, 75 Mile House and so on.

West of Cache Creek, where the Fraser and the Thompson rivers meet, is Kamloops, the major centre of the Thompson, Nicola, Lillooet and Southern Cariboo regions. Kamloops, which began as a Hudson's Bay trading fort in 1821, has had many distinguished citizens, but none made an entry into the community as dramatic as did Rose Schubert, who arrived in Kamloops – and the world – on October 14, 1862. Rose's mother, Catherine, had been the only woman in a party of about 200 who had decided to journey overland in that year to the B.C. gold diggings. The British Columbia Overland Transit Company promised them "the speediest, safest and most economical route" to the diggings across the open prairies of the West and through the mountains. By the time the party had reached Fort Gary by steamer, their number had dropped to 135. With Captain Thomas McMicking as their leader,

the party loaded up their Red River carts and the journey began in earnest.

The Overlanders, which included the pregnant Mrs. Schubert, her husband and their three children, reached Fort Edmonton on July 21. Here, another ten members of the party thought the junket was not for them and dropped out. The rest of the group made their painstaking way through the Rockies, not reaching Tête Jaune Cache (named for a fair-haired Metis trapper called Pierre Hatsinaton (Tête Jaune) who used to store furs and supplies here in the 1800s) until August 27. With almost all their food gone, the party decided to split into two. The larger group built rafts and rode the rapids and the canyons of the Fraser to Quesnel.

Below: Canada Pavilion seen from Granville Square, and (facing page) the impressive glass dome of the Bloedel Conservatory.

Miraculously, all but one arrived on September 11.

The twenty people who made up the smaller group included the Schubert family. After enduring great hardships, they reached Fort Kamloops on October 13. The following day the indomitable Mrs. Schubert gave birth to Rose, the first white child born in the B.C. interior.

Today, the spectacular Yellowhead Highway traces the route of the Overlanders of '62. North Thompson country is as diverse as it is breathtaking. Vast forests, echoing waterfalls, silent volcanoes, mineral springs, sparkling mountain lakes teeming with kokanee salmon and brook, rainbow, steelhead, and Kamloops trout all await visitors to this natural wonderland. Unparalleled wilderness experiences beckon seasoned backpackers and hikers in Wells Gray Provincial Park, site of the glistening Helmcken Falls, and Mount Robson Provincial Park, preserve of over 200,000 hectares of snowcapped mountains, precipitous canyons, glacier-fed lakes, wild rivers and forested valleys. Not to be missed is the 22-kilometre Berg Lake Trail that runs from the Yellowhead Highway through the Valley of a Thousand Falls to Berg Lake.

Many glaciers can be seen along the way including Berg Glacier, which is about 1800m thick and almost a kilometre wide. Above the lake towers mighty Mount Robson, at 3954m the highest peak in the Rockies. The deepest cave in Canada, Arctomys Cave, lies in a valley of Mount Robson. Only very experienced spelunkers should attempt the 2400-metre passage to the bottom of Arctomys.

Standing in noble salute to a gallant young British Columbian is Mount Terry Fox. Having lost one leg to cancer, Terry Fox decided to raise money for cancer research by running a "Marathon for Hope" across Canada. Fox began his run at St. John's, Newfoundland, on April 12, 1980, but was forced to end it on

Left: Robson Square and the elegant new Vancouver Art Gallery. Overleaf: (left) the vast, yet graceful, Lions Gate Bridge, and (right) sunrise over Burrard Inlet, spanned by Second Narrows Bridge.

September 1 in Thunder Bay, Ontario, when it was discovered that he had cancer of the lungs. In those few months he ran 5373km, covering an average of 40km a day. Terry Fox died at New Westminster on June 28, 1981. His heroic run raised over $23 million for cancer research.

Closer to Kamloops, north-east of Savona Provincial Park is Deadman Valley, one of the hottest and driest areas of British Columbia. This is prickly pear and sagebrush country. On the road through Deadman Valley – named for a Nor'Wester who was killed here by his Indian companion sometime around 1815 – to the town of Cultus Creek, a multi-colored cliff formation rises some 60m from the Deadman River. Split Rock, as it's called, is fretted with caves and fissures. Fine agates and petrified wood samples can be found on the cliffs, which are volcanic in origin. Beyond Split Rock stands the most curious feature of Deadman Valley – five hoodoos. These eroded pinacles of rock and clay conglomerate are almost 12m high. Each is topped by an overhanging capstone, making them look rather like five giant, prehistoric mushrooms.

Clinging to the sides of the hills along the Thompson River Valley before you turn off to go to Cultus Lake is an old irrigation flume, a poignant reminder of a short time when orchards and hope blossomed in this dry land. In the early 1900s, the Marquis of Anglesey combined his wealth with the Yankee ingenuity of a Mr. Charles Barnes in a scheme to irrigate the tableland above the Thompson in order to plant orchards.

Water was brought from Snohoosh Lake, north of the Deadman Valley, by means of miles of wooden flume and irrigation ditches. By 1911, a large area of land had been irrigated and a townsite called Walhachin (Indian for "abundant land") had been built on the south bank of the river. The first crop of Jonathan apples was shipped to market in 1913. Corn, tomatoes, onions, tobacco and beans were also planted in this new Garden of Eden. Then World War I broke out. All but ten of Walhachin's young settlers went off to fight for king and country. Maintaining the irrigation system was more work than those left behind could cope with. So the fruit

trees drooped from lack of water and the crops perished. And the sagebrush gradually crept back and took over. All that's left of that brave experiment that war killed is the little village of Walhachin and a few gnarled apple trees that, each April, manage to blossom amongst the sagebrush.

About 90km west of Kamloops is Ashcroft, long known as the "copper capital of Canada." South of Ashcroft, at Lytton, the Fraser and Thompson rivers converge, as the mighty, murky Fraser swallows up the blue-green Thompson all within a distance of less than 50m. Jade fanciers will likely find searching the river beds at Lytton quite rewarding.

If you follow the Fraser south past Boston Bar, you'll come to Hell's Gate. Here the Fraser Canyon is at its narrowest – not quite 30m across. Unlike Simon Fraser and his party, who had to inch their way along the canyon above the seething waters aided only by an Indian-constructed network of ropes, modern travellers can cross the Fraser's gorge in the Hell's Gate Airtram. The gorge is 180m deep, and with the Fraser thundering through it at more than 7m a second, the Airtram's descent into the canyon is a trip no one can ever forget.

Hell's Gate was also the site of a disastrous rockslide in 1914. The slide, which severely constricted the channel, resulted in part from railway construction. The slide prevented thousands of sockeye salmon from reaching their spawning grounds, with disastrous consequences for the fishing industry. In 1944 fishladders were built here to permit the spawning fish to bypass the turbulent rapids.

Once past Spuzzum and Yale, with its lovely, wooden, Anglican Church of St. John the Divine (B.C.'s oldest

Above: the Royal Vancouver Yacht Club in Horseshoe Bay. Facing page: traffic-congested Lions Gate Bridge. Overleaf: (right) the Princess Patricia at Coal Harbour in Burrard Inlet (left).

house of worship still on its original site), and Hope, the Fraser breaks out of its mountain fastness. Now it flows serenely through the broad flood plain that stretches for about 100km from Chilliwack to the Pacific Ocean. Massive silt deposits, the accumulation of 50 million years, make the lower Fraser Valley one of the richest agricultural regions in Canada.

Fittingly, at the mouth of this historic river is Vancouver, Canada's third largest city and her gateway to the twenty-first century.

While all roads do eventually lead to Vancouver and following the Fraser to get there is an ideal route, in

Facing page: boats on the blue waters of Vancouver's Horseshoe Bay, and (above) Canada Place against a burnished sky.

a province as large as B.C., there are always other roads beckoning. An alternate route from Kamloops goes southeast on Highway 97 and winds through the lovely, fertile Okanagan Valley.

The Okanagan Valley is actually a deep gorge scoured in a large plateau that stretches between the Cascade and Monashee mountain ranges. First inhabited by the Okanagan and Shuswap Indians, the area was explored by a small group of fur traders led by David Stuart in 1811. Stuart was in the employ of the American-owned Pacific Fur Company.

Settlement did not begin in the Okanagan until 1859. In that year, French-born Father Charles Pandosy, an Oblate priest, arrived with two other priests and four settlers. He established a mission is Kelowna, where it may still be seen on the corner of Benvoulin and Casorso roads. The first winter saw the little group at the mission reduced to eating moss and roots. But they persevered, and less than fifteen years later, the mission could boast of a fine orchard, vegetable garden, cattle, chickens, ducks and geese. Father Pandosy is said to have brought the first apple trees and the first grape vines to the Okanagan.

Lord Aberdeen, a later Governor-General of Canada, and his very enterprising wife were responsible for giving commercial orcharding in the Okanagan its strongest impetus. These Scottish aristocrats began growing apples commercially in 1892 on their properties in Kelowna and Vernon. The latter location also became the site of the Aberdeens' jam-making enterprise. To encourage the growing of fruit, Lord and Lady Aberdeen subdivided their vast Vernon holding, the Coldstream Ranch, into smaller, reasonably priced orchards which were offered to prospective settlers. The Canadian government and the Canadian Pacific Railway also supported the fledgling orchard community by providing settlers passage from England to the Okanagan for just $40.

Today, irrigation, fertile soil and a mild climate mean that one-third of all the apples eaten in Canada come from the Okanagan. But the Okanagan is more than just apples – from the first cherries in June, the following months mean an abundant supply of apricots, peaches, pears, plums, nectarines and melons.

Okanagan's warm, dry climate, so similar to that of Germany's Rhine Valley, nourishes B.C.'s outstanding vineyards. Although winemaking in the Okanagan just dates from the inception of Calona Wines in 1932, the output of both commercial and estate wineries alike has earned wide praise from oenophiles. Many wineries are open for tours, from the Brights House of Wines at Oliver, the most automated winery in the valley, and the Divino Estate Winery, also near Oliver, to the Claremont Estate Winery at Peachland, the valley's first estate winery, and Calona Wines in Kelowna, B.C.'s first successful entry into the competitive U.S. market.

Nature has been so good to the Okanagan. Its peaceful, prosperous towns like Armstrong, Summerland, Penticton, Vernon and Enderby thrive in this land of bountiful lakes and guardian mountains. With the southern part of the valley given over to fruit, the northern end of the Okanagan is dairy country, renowned throughout the world for its excellent cheeses. With so much of the bounty of the good earth to hand – you can buy freshly picked fruit at little roadside stalls throughout the valley – you'd be advised to head off down a secluded country road and find yourself your own little lake just made for a well-

stocked picnic hamper and a long, lazy afternoon of doing nothing. However, if you're anywhere near Okanagan Lake, be careful – or watchful, or both. For the lake is the legendary home of Ogopogo, the valley's very own monster. Ogopogo is reasonably easy to recognize – he's between 9 and 21m long and has a head rather like a horse's – or a sheep's – or a goats! (Ogopogo's a pretty fast swimmer, too, which may

Below: the city seen from Cypress Provincial Park. Facing page: the Macmillan Planetarium, with Grouse Mountain in the background.

account for the garbled description of his features.)

Next door to the Okanagan Valley is the Kootenay Region. Silver put the Kootenays on the map. In 1882 the Blue Bell silver-lead mine near Nelson was opened. Similar finds were made in the Slocan area, while copper was discovered at Phoenix. The real rush to the Kootenays followed the dramatic 1895 rise in the price of silver on international markets.

Like the Cariboo gold rush, the discovery of silver in the Kootenays also brought a stampede of fortune seekers to the area. However, mining in the Kootenays called for heavily capitalized, large-scale operations, so most of the would-be Billy Barkers ended up as wage earners. Here in the rough-and-ready towns that they built – places like Rossland and Sandon, Grand Forks and Slocan City – was nourished much of the ardent unionism so characteristic of west coast labour.

Incidentally, Grand Forks also became home to another group of newcomers who were more interested in farming than mining. The Doukhobors, religious dissenters from Tsarist Russia, followed their leader Peter Verigin west from the Prairies to farm here in the early 1900s. Mountain View, a restored Doukhobor farm house dating from 1912, allows visitors to get a glimpse into the world of these industrious and often controversial settlers.

Many of the early silver towns are no more, but their ghostly remnants may be found throughout the area, surrendering silently to the en- circling forest.

Spectacular scenery makes the Kootenay region a favourite with photographers. Its many brilliant blue lakes are stocked with some of the biggest rainbow trout to be found anywhere. Dolly Varden and kokanee salmon are also plentiful.

Attractions not to be missed in the Kootenays include the Cody Caves, especially the Throne Room, a marvellous limestone gallery of stalactites and stalagmites and long, hollow fingers of calcium known as soda straws; and the refreshing, mineral-rich waters of the Ainsworth Hot Springs, the perfect total body restorative after a hard day's sight-seeing.

Winter transforms the Kootenays into a snowy playground. Some of the best skiing in the province is to be found around Nelson, a town also noted for its many impressive, ornate buildings dating from the early mining boom days.

B.C.'s first hydro-electric plant was built at Cottonwood Falls, near Nelson, in 1896. Today, under the terms of the Columbia River Treaty (1961), there is a chain of dams along the Columbia River that provides power to B.C. and the U.S.

Swinging west from Grand Forks, Highway 3 passes through Greenwood. Some 2,500 Japanese-Canadians were moved here after being expelled from their homes on the West Coast in 1941. The Japanese artifacts on display at the Greenwood Museum offer silent testimony to one of B.C.'s least-proud moments.

Highway 3 from Osoyoos to Tashme starts off in dense rain forests and ends up passing through desert where the chief vegetation is prickly pear. Irrigation is responsible for the bountiful orchards of the Osoyoos.

The old Dewdney Trail, built by engineer Edward Dewdney in the 1860s to connect Hope, on the Fraser River, with the Kootenay region, is faithfully followed by Highway 3 between Keremeos and Princeton and Manning Provincial Park and Tashme.

Years ago, Indians used to come from as far away as the Prairies to present-day Princeton to trade with the local Salish tribes for vermilion, which was much prized for war paint. You can still see Vermilion Bluffs, the source of this red ocher, about 3km up the Tulameen River from Princeton.

Manning Provincial Park, with its towering peaks, is popular with nature lovers in all seasons, but it's particularly inviting in July and August, when shy, alpine yellow snow lilies, Indian hellebores and towhead babies or anemones turn the park's Blackwall Peak into a magic carpet of many colors.

Whether you follow the Fraser into Vancouver or divert through the Okanagan Valley, B.C.'s endlessly

Grouse Mountain Skyride (right) offers superb views of Vancouver and its surrounding scenery.

changing landscape makes for some of the most breathtaking and exciting travel experiences on the North American continent.

But B.C. is more than just spectacular scenery, it's the habitat of countless creatures as varied as the terrains in which they live. If you begin the roll call of B.C.'s furred, feathered and aquatic life in the rain forests of the west coast, you'll find black-tailed deer, elk, wolves, black bears and cougars. Stellar's jays, red-crested pileated woodpeckers and Swainson's thrushes like these moist woods, as do blue grouse, whose strange, hollow booming is one of nature's great diversionary tactics. You can hear it plainly, but you can never tell just where the sound is coming from.

White-tailed deer roam the wet forests of the interior along with mule deer and moose. In the winter, northern caribou seek shelter in these forests, and food in the form of tree lichens.

Most birds shun B.C.'s harsh alpine zone, but not the white-tailed ptarmigan, the water pipit, the mountain chickadee, Brewer's sparrow or the strident Clark's nutcracker. Like the mammals of B.C.'s north – grizzly bears, woodland caribou, bighorn sheep and the beautiful, white mountain goat – these birds are quite at home in this harsh terrain.

Subalpine forests are moose territory, but mule deer, wolves, bears and lynx are also part of this ecosystem. Birds of the region include boreal chickadees, bohemian waxwings, spruce grouse and evening grosbeaks.

Moose also forage in the boreal forest during the winter. Other residents include black and grizzly bears, porcupines, beavers, coyotes, muskrats, timber wolves, lynx and martens. The boreal forest is a favourite summer habitat of robins, jays, grouse, warblers and kinglets. The swamps and marshy lakes of the boreal provide sheltered nesting sites for waterfowl and red-winged blackbirds and are the permanent domain of the boreal owl.

Below: the lights of Canada Place sparkling as the sun sets, and (facing page) downtown buildings reflecting the colours of the sunrise.

Many bird species nest in the Caribou-Chilcotin region: ruddy ducks, grebes, coots, mallards, teals, shovellers, American wigeons, loons, goldeneye ducks and phalaropes, to name just a few. One of B.C.'s endangered birds, the white pelican, nests only on Stum Lake in the Chilcotin. Birdwatchers should also look for lazuli buntings, western kingbirds, mountain bluebirds and yellow-bellied sapsuckers. Common mammals include badgers, moose, mule deer, bears, yellow-bellied marmots and jumping mice.

Mourning doves and kestrels are everywhere in the Okanagan, Similkameen and Thompson valleys, contentedly perched atop telephone wires and posts of any size. The white-throated swift and the white-headed woodpecker may be spotted, if you're extremely fortunate. Much easier to sight are the western tanager, American redstart, lazuli bunting, nuthatch and yellow-breasted chat.

Where sagebrush now rules in the Fraser, Thompson, Okanagan, Nicola and Similikameen drainage areas, lush bunchgrass – "higher than a horse's belly" – once used to grow. Grazing has eliminated most of this grass cover, but where it exists you'll find horned larks and western meadowlarks, magpies, nighthawks and long-billed curlews. The mighty golden eagle and the handsome red-tailed hawk race the skies here. The calliope hummingbird, Canada's smallest bird, is also to be found in this terrain, feeding off the thistles that it loves so much.

Facing page: a football match inside Vancouver's vast British Columbia Place Stadium (below).

Coyotes like sagebrush country, as do gophers, badgers and a number of different lizards and snakes, including rattlesnakes. In the hot, dry south of these valleys, where rainfall averages less than 20cm a year, live mountain cottontail rabbits, pocket mice, and rare, white-tailed jackrabbit and pallid bats. Black widow spiders and painted turtles are some of the other creatures that have adapted to life in this difficult terrain. Perhaps the best-known inhabitants here are those necessary scavengers, the much maligned, bald-headed turkey vulture.

B.C.'s waters also teem with life. Indeed, for every Canadian who thinks B.C. means mountains and lumber, two more will tell you fish is what the province is all about.

There are five species of Pacific ocean salmon – coho, chinook, sockeye, chum and pink. Salmon are anadromous fish. Although they hatch in river gravels, they spend most of their adult lives in the ocean. Just what brings salmon back to their ancestral streams to spawn and die, and how they manage to find the spot where they were born remains a mystery.

Kokanee salmon, found so plentifully in the Kootenays, spend their lives in lakes rather than the sea, but they, too, return to their original streams to spawn.

Surely one of the most marvellous sights to be seen in B.C. is the Fraser River sockeye salmon run. Every October for three weeks, millions of sockeye salmon, their bodies changed from slivery blue to blood red, swim furiously up the Fraser and Thompson rivers, covering up to 50km a day, to spawn in a few hectares of gravel in the Adams River. Then, days later, their life cycle over, the fish wither away and die.

Other important ocean fish are herring, whose roe is valued as a delicacy in Japan, giant halibut, sole, brill, cod and turbot.

Of the sixty of so freshwater species, trout (rainbow and cutthroat) and char (Dolly Varden and lake trout) are the best known and most popular with anglers, as

Previous pages: colourful boats in Vancouver Harbour, and (left) Granville Island Market.

indeed is the feisty steelhead. Other freshwater species include gray or lake trout, mountain whitefish and white sturgeon. Northern pike, walleye and Arctic grayling are found only in the waters of B.C.'s north.

B.C. tidelife is rich in oysters, shrimp and many types of clams. And there are more varieties of starfish to be found on the B.C. coast than anywhere else in the world!

Depending on location, the mammals and birds of B.C.'s shores run the full gamut of rowdy gulls and great blue herons to black oyster-catchers, sanderlings and those sociable communal feeders, the dunlin. B.C.'s remote islands provide nesting sites for innumerable species, including pigeon guillemots, tufted puffins, Leach's storm-petrels, rhinoceros auklets and common murres. The isolated cliffs of the Queen Charlottes are favoured by Peale's peregrine falcon, the world's fastest-flying bird.

Sea mammals include killer whales, harbour seals, dall porpoises and sea lions – the original gregarious sun worshippers.

Not quite two centuries ago, Captain George Vancouver reflected on this new land with the following entry in his log: "To describe the beauties of this region, will, on some future occasion be a grateful task to the pen of a skillful panygyrist. The serenity of the climate, the innumerable pleasing landscapes and the abundant fertility that nature puts forth, require only to be enriched by the industry of man with villages, mansions, cottages and other buildings, to render it the most lovely country that can be imagined." Although Vancouver was talking about the island that bears his name, his remarks apply equally to all B.C. Yet some would argue that the "industry of man" has come perilously close to ruining what is the most lovely country imaginable. And it's true that greed and carelessness have depleted fish stocks, reduced once mighty forests to characterless woods, turned grasslands into near desert and senselessly squandered mineral riches.

In a province so recently settled, progress and newness at all costs have occasionally seemed to be B.C.'s main reason for existence.

If this attitude has taken its toll of B.C.'s natural resources, its human cost has also been high. Following a pattern all too common in North America, B.C.'s Indians have paid the greatest price for the province's prosperity.

In the early days of B.C.'s history, the insatiable demands of the logging industry and, to a lesser extent, of the fishing industry, combined with the push of settlement, led increasingly to wholesale expropriation of traditional Indian territory. The coming of the railway and Confederation, seen as harbingers of a new age of progress and wealth for most British Columbians, brought the province's first citizens nothing. Made wards of the federal government and confined to reservations, the Indians saw their claims for just land settlements bandied back and forth between the provincial and federal jurisdictions.

Settlement, when it finally came in the 1920s, gave the Indians less than 0.4 percent of the vast province which once had been theirs. The Indian campaign to get the provincial government to redress these persistent wrongs continues to this

Below: the new Vancouver Art Gallery on Robson Square, and (facing page) the Pan Pacific Hotel at Canada Place.

day.

The ugly face of racism has also more than once showed itself in B.C. The Chinese, who had arrived in the province with the gold miners from California in 1858, were the first recipients of racial bigotry.

During the 1870s, labour contractors brought over Chinese men to work as farm labourers, domestics and in the fish canneries. Repeated moves to halt Chinese immigration were foiled by the labour demands of the Canadian Pacific Railway. If the railway was to go through, the much-exploited Chinese were essential. Declared Prime Minister Sir John A. Macdonald: "Either you have this labour or you can't have the railway." B.C. got the point, and in 1882, railway contractor Andrew Onderdonk imported 6,000 Chinese labourers to work on the railway. Working for $1 a day, at dangerous jobs whites would not do, the Chinese enabled the railway to be built, and ahead of time too. So little interest was taken in their well-being, however, that to this day, while we know that many Chinese died building the railway, no-one knows just how many.

In later years the imposition of headtaxes, as much as $100 in 1901, were designed to restrict further Chinese immigration. Official discrimination of this kind did not end until the 1960s, and over the years lent a certain legitimacy to the periodic anti-Chinese riots that broke out in major settlements.

The Japanese, who arrived later than the Chinese, in the 1890s, were to fare even worse. Their efforts in the fishing industry were met with great hostility. But it was Pearl Harbour that ushered in the darkest stain on British Columbia's history. On February 26, 1942, over 23,000 Japanese British Columbians, both native-born and immigrants, were expelled from their homes on the coast and settled in camps in the B.C. hinterland. Their property was confiscated and sold for a song. No charge of treason was ever proved against these much-wronged British Columbians, who even now still seek compensation for this loss of their rights and property.

Today's B.C. glories in its ethnic diversity, as multicultural Vancouver and other centres and communities

Above: a ship against the setting sun on English Bay, and (facing page) the lights of the Expo 86 site, with Grouse Mountain beyond.

around the province so richly and vibrantly attest.

Like the American west coast, British Columbia has a young history. The baby of the Canadian family (somehow Newfoundland, which only joined Confederation in 1949, doesn't count, the nation's story having begun here centuries before), British Columbia sometimes seems like a precocious child, launched too hastily into jaded adult company. B.C. has basked in the applause of its elders and realized, only too late, the lack of substance behind the praise. The province has been burnt by the experience. As a result, there's mistrust and resentment here of Eastern Canada, seen as the source of much of B.C.'s exploitation. For all it's a land of vast natural resources and limited population, B.C. feels acutely the periodic slumps in world markets for these resources. Unemployment in Canada hurts more keenly here in terms of numbers than in industrialized Ontario, for example.

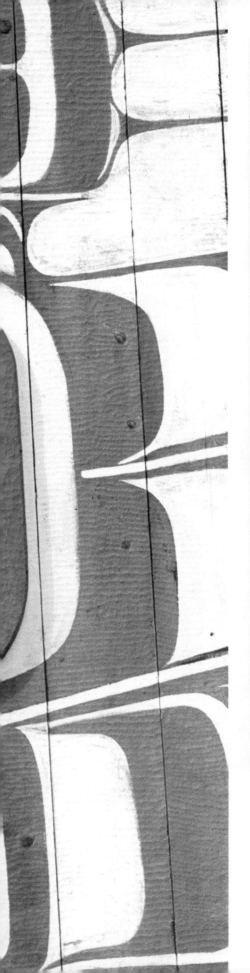

Among the legacies left by the Northwest Pacific Coast Indians is their unique and powerful style of wood carving. Totem poles (above, left and top inset) were designed as crests of a family or clan and, whilst they were primarily symbols of prestige, they could also be functional, serving as doorposts or memorials for relatives. This beautiful art form also included the carving and painting of canoes, houses and masks. Overleaf: Granville Island and the imposing Burrard Bridge.

In spite of, or perhaps because of, these past conditions, today's more mature B.C. is determined to tread its own course and establish a more secure base on which to build economic stability.

British Columbians have always been people of tomorrow. Their great pride in their province and confidence in its future, so evident in the bold innovations of Expo '86, still justify George Brown's famous Confederation remark that British Columbia is "the land of golden opportunities."

Facing page: the downtown area, with English Bay beyond. Below: the city skyline sparkles against the Coast Mountains.

At the time Vancouver came into being as a city in April 6, 1886, Halifax in Nova Scotia had been well-established for over a century. As cities go, young Vancouver was downright ugly, being not much more than a collection of shacks; very much the poor Cinderella beside gracious Victoria on neighboring Vancouver Island. The analogy doesn't end there, for Vancouver's early history shows it to have been merely an afterthought. In fact, if it hadn't been for the foresight of Sir William Van Horne, Canada's railway czar, Vancouver might never have existed at all.

Early explorers of B.C.'s west coast, be they Spaniards or England's intrepid sea captains Cook and Vancouver, all found the land that is now Vancouver Island, across the Strait of Georgia from mainland B.C., more appealing as a potential site of settlement. Vancouver's comments on the site of the city that was to bear his name were dry and to the point: "The shores... (were) of a moderate height, and though rocky, well covered with trees of large growth, principally of the pine tree." Hardly prose designed to stimulate a population stampede.

Fur traders followed the explorers, but it was gold that actually provided the impetus for developing the territory we now know as British Columbia. The great Cariboo gold rush of 1858-59 turned Victoria, at the southern tip of Vancouver Island,

Above: Vancouver at sunset. Facing page: the Bloedel Conservatory and the colourful Sunken Gardens in Queen Elizabeth Park.

and tiny Fort Langley, a Hudson's Bay Company fur fort situated on the mainland about 50km (30 miles) from the mouth of the Fraser River, into boom towns. Mainland British Columbia became a British colony with New Westminister as its capital. And what did gold mean to Vancouver? Directly, nothing. Indirectly, gold or the lack of it, forced three young, failed prospectors to decide that maybe there was money to be made providing the new boom towns with much needed building supplies. People laughed and called John Morton, William Hailstone and Samuel Brighouse the "Three Greenhorns" when, in 1862, they pre-empted some 200 hectares (about 500 acres) near Burrard Inlet (the site with all the pine trees Captain Vancouver had observed back in

1792). Their land contained coal and a seam of clay suitable for making bricks. Incidentally, the "Brickmakers' Claim," as it was known, took up what is now the entire West End of Vancouver: real estate worth millions!

Some time in the 1860s farming began on the southern section of Burrard Peninsula near the Fraser River. In the end, though, logging really got Vancouver off the ground. The easily accessible timber of Burrard Inlet and English Bay led to the opening, in 1863, of Pioneer Mills. The first delivery of lumber from the mill went to New Westminster on August 12, 1863.

A year later, the *Ellen Lewis* left for Australia with a cargo of Burrard Inlet timber.

By the end of the 1860s, the lumber

trade with Australia, San Francisco and South America was thriving, providing work for the small white population and the indigenous Musqueam and Squamish Indians.

Pioneer Mills didn't enjoy a monopoly on the lumber trade. In 1865, Captain Edward Stamp had built a sawmill on the South Shore. Clustered around Stamp's Mill was a little shacktown for the mill workers. A similar community, called Moodyville after the mill's owner, clung to the North Shore mill. In addition to being examples of primitive living at its best, these two communities had one thing in common – they were

both dry as a whistle.

Now logging is thirsty work, a fact not lost on a former sailor-prospector-steamboatman turned saloonkeeper by the name of Captain John "Gassy Jack" Deighton. In 1867, Deighton built a saloon just west of Stamp's Mill. The building, a 3.5m x 7.5m shack (about 12'x24') was constructed in less than a day, thanks to the assistance of Jack's future patrons, who totally approved of the enterprise. Soon a little village, basically as rustic as the saloon, grew up around Gassy Jack's. (Deighton acquired his nickname from his habit of talking – or gassing – too much.) By 1870, Gastown, as the village had originally been called, covered six blocks, and had been rechristened Granville.

The future, however, did not seem too rosy for Gastown/Granville – and indeed for the whole of lower mainland British Columbia. The gold rush was over; Victoria had succeeded in wresting capital city

status away from New Westminster, and the lumber market – Burrard Inlet's *raison d'etre* – was always in a state of flux.

Confederation and the railway were to save Granville and ultimately make the city's future, though at the time, just the opposite seemed likely to happen.

When British Columbia joined the Canadian Confederation in 1871, the province did so on the understanding that the Pacific would be linked to the Atlantic by a transcontinental railroad. This railroad was to be finished in 1881. Various routes were suggested, with the choice of the final terminus being all important. An initial route proposed having the railroad reach the coast at Bute Inlet. From here it would bridge Seymour Narrows, and come down Vancouver Island to its terminus at Victoria.

A later plan called for a route down the Fraser Valley to the head of Burrard Inlet. The first route spelled riches for Victoria; the second, for

Above: a Sea Bus crossing Burrard Inlet towards Canada Pavilion. Facing page: the glittering orb of the Expo Centre. Overleaf: aerial views of Simon Frazer University, revealing its attractive layout.

Port Moody. Both meant oblivion for Granville.

While rivalry between the mainland and Vancouver Island over the routes intensified, the future of the railway itself was seriously imperilled by scandals concerning the improper awarding of construction contracts.

Finally, Prime Minister Sir John A. Macdonald settled on the Fraser Valley/Port Moody route – much to Victoria's chagrin – and work commenced on the British Columbia section of the Canadian Pacific Railway in May 1880.

In 1881, William Van Horne, described by an admirer as "the ablest railroad general in the world,

all that Grant was to the U.S.A.," was appointed general manager of the Canadian Pacific Railway. For Granville, the consequences of this appointment were to be enormous.

In August 1884 Van Horne visited Granville and decided that this was to be the site of the CPR western terminus, rather than Port Moody, some 19km (12 miles) to the east. Business, not sentiment, dictated Van Horne's decision. The lack of abundant flat land suitable for industry and railyards around Port Moody, combined with the port's tidal flats and its treacherous entrance for shipping through the Second Narrows, made Port Moody undesirable as the terminus for the CPR.

The unusual, sail-like roof of Canada Pavilion (these pages) is an eye-catching spectacle by both night and day.

Van Horne decided that Granville was not a sufficiently grand appellation for a mighty railway terminus, and is said to have rechristened the community on the spot by declaring: "I name thee Vancouver." Van Horne felt the new name would mean something to people back home in Great Britain, who would connect the name with their social studies lessons on Captain Vancouver and Vancouver Island.

Victorians, still smarting under the Port Moody incident, were incensed over this later development. Not only did they stand to lose their pre-eminent economic position to this upstart mainland town, they stood to lose their very identity as well. Protests were in vain. Perhaps anticipating the hopelessness of their case, shrewd Victorians went shopping for land in Vancouver, even while they cried "foul" in the legislature.

When Lord Strathcona drove the railroad's famous "last spike" at Craigellaichie in the Monashee Mountain range on November 7, 1885, Vancouver's future as the premier west coast city was assured. On May 3, 1886 Mayor Maclean proudly addressed the city's first Council meeting: "We commence today... to lay the foundation of a city which is destined... to take a prominent place among the most progressive cities... of Canada. Before many years pass...(we shall be) second only to San Francisco on the Pacific Coast." Considering that San Francisco had a population of more than 250,000, whereas there were only about 600 Vancouverites, skeptics might have been forgiven for doubting the accuracy of Maclean's vision.

A month later, on Sunday June 13, fire raged through the young city. In forty-five minutes Vancouver was nothing but a pile of ashes. But catas-

trophe was not to stop Vancouver. Reconstruction began the following day, even as smoke drifted lazily in the air above the blackened, scorched site.

Six months later, Vancouver was a bustling city where citizens could enjoy all the amenities afforded by 23 hotels, 51 stores, 14 office blocks, 2 stables, 9 saloons, a bank, church, hospital, opera house and a grand, two-storey city hall. Five months later, on May 23, 1887, the first transcontinental train arrived in Vancouver. It was a great day for the people of Vancouver. Over 2,000 of them turned out to cheer Engine No. 374 as she steamed into the depot, garlanded with flowers, her headlight bearing a portrait of Queen Victoria – 1887 was her Majesty's golden jubilee. Wrapped around the engine's smokestack was a big banner that proclaimed: "Montreal Greets the Terminal City."

The wisdom of Van Horne's choice of Vancouver over Port Moody became instantly apparent less than

Below: a view across False Creek towards the magnificent North Shore Mountains. Facing page: a marina in Horseshoe Bay.

a month later, when the CPR-chartered steamer *Abyssinia* docked at Vancouver from Yokohama, Japan on June 14. The *Abyssinia*'s cargo of tea and silk was then carried by the railway to waiting eastern markets in Montreal, Chicago and New York. And so was started the vital trans-Pacific trade links that today make Vancouver probably the most important commercial centre in Canada.

One hundred years later, when Vancouver invited the world to help celebrate its centenary at its giant party, the 1986 World's Fair, the city paid tribute to those transport pioneers whose foresight and daring had put Vancouver on the map. The focus of Expo '86, held in Vancouver from May 2, 1986 to October 13, 1986, was transportation and its natural off-shoot, communication.

The years between Vancouver's birth and its centennial celebrations brought the usual mix of boom and gloom experienced by most growing cities. The depression of 1893, which hit Vancouver hard, was soon forgotten in the good economic times that followed the discovery of gold in the Klondike in 1897. The great San Francisco earthquake of 1906 caused a run on B.C. lumber, which was needed for the city's reconstruction. Fish canneries, opened up on the coast and the Fraser River during the 1880s and 1890s, fed a huge export market in Eastern Canada, Australia and Great Britain. B.C.'s rich mineral resources in copper, zinc, silver as well as gold also contributed to Vancouver's increasing commercial dominance.

World War I put the lid on Vancouver's growth, but only temporarily. Prosperity returned with the post war years, aided by the arrival of the Canadian Northern Railway and the opening of the Panama Canal, which brought new trade possibilities for Vancouver. Immigrants

Below: the skyline from Kitsilano Yacht Club, and (facing page) an aerial view of Queen Elizabeth Park and the Bloedel Conservatory.

Facing page: an view of the downtown district, and (above) Canada Place at dusk. Overleaf: aerial views over (right) False Creek, and (left) the flat roof of Eaton's department store and surrounding downtown buildings.

flocked to this province of hope, enriching B.C. even as they prospered themselves. Many of these newcomers came to Vancouver, and by 1929 the population of Greater Vancouver numbered around 300,000 people.

Then came the Great Depression. Vancouver suffered greatly. Then as now, Vancouver has always had to provide assistance not only for its own unemployed but for those from other parts of the province and the rest of Canada, drawn to the city by its mild climate. By December 1935, Vancouver was almost bankrupt.

The outbreak of World War II helped restore Vancouver's sagging fortunes. The war, in particular the invasion of Pearl Harbour, also resurrected one of Vancouver's darker sides – racism. Although Vancouver's Chinese, Japanese, and East Indians had been the victims of ugly discrimination and hostility in the past, this treatment paled in comparison to the shameful abuse of Japanese Canadians during the war.

The war's end restored Vancouver's equilibrium and ushered in a period of economic resurgence. Today, with a population of over one-and one-quarter million and growing fast, metropolitan Vancouver stretches in all directions, taking in the communities of North Vancouver, Port Coquitlam, Port Moody, Richmond, Burnaby, Surrey, White Rock, Delta, Lions Bay, Pitt Meadows, Langley City, Langley and New Westminster.

Like San Francisco or Sydney, Australia, or Rio de Janeiro, Vancouver is one of the world's most splendidly situated cities. You can see the mountains or the sea in the

distance from almost every street in this multi-level city of beaches, parks, highrises, still higher mountains and expansive heavens. Surrounded by so much natural beauty, Vancouverites are keenly in tune with nature. This love for following the rhythms of nature shows in their unhurried lifestyles. Sensible Vancouverites set their own pace and are known to take an occasional afternoon off for a dip in the Pacific at Kitsilano Beach or a sail on beautiful English Bay. After-work skiing on illuminated Grouse Mountain, just twenty minutes from the city, is an everyday part of winter life.

Hikers, and there are many here, regularly don backpack and boots to explore the trails of the Coast Mountains behind the city. Sunday-afternoon walkers, just about all Vancouverites and not just on Sundays either, have over 140 parks to choose from. The largest of these parks is beautiful Stanley Park. Originally a military reserve, Stanley Park was acquired from the federal government and dedicated by Governor-General Lord Stanley as a park intended "for the use and enjoyment of peoples of all colours, creeds and customs" in 1889. The park, which is situated on a peninsula jutting out into Burrard Inlet, covers some 400 hectares (1000 acres) and includes Canada's largest aquarium, a zoo, beaches, beautiful gardens, pony rides, and a miniature railway. Live theatre is staged in the park during the summer months.

Marvellous views of the city can be had from Queen Elizabeth Park on top of Little Mountain, the highest point within the city limits. The Van Dusen Botanical Gardens contain Vancouver's largest collection of trees, shrubs, plants and flowers. But perhaps the loveliest of Vancouver's parks is the Nitobe Memorial Gardens, on the north-western edge of the University of British Columbia. This tranquil, authentic Japanese garden is complete with bonsai, a teahouse and a snow temple.

Although Vancouver was not laid out according to any grand plan, it has always attracted innovative architects, whose eclectic styles, both past

Above: the night skyline dominated by the circular observation deck of the Harbour Centre (overleaf left), (facing page) yachts moored in False Creek and Coal Harbour, and (overleaf right) the bright lights of Granville Street.

and present, have made the cityscape so vibrantly diverse.

Unfortunately, some fine old Vancouver landmarks fell victim to the wrecker's ball long before the present trend toward preserving the past as the heritage of the future took root in Vancouver. Sadly missing is the handsome, Nordic-styled, turreted station that the Canadian Pacific Railway built at the foot of Granville Street at the turn of the century, and the McLeery farm house, the city's first pioneer residence. This fine old clapboard building, one of the few to survive the great fire of 1886, was demolished to make way for a golf course in 1955.

The elaborately classical Pantages Theatre, a famous, and infamous, vaudeville haunt on West Hastings Street, also is no more, demolished to

Above: tower blocks against snow-capped mountains seen from Vanier Park, Vancouver. Facing page: a forest of masts in False Creek.

clear space for a parking lot.

Salutes to the past like the flatiron Hotel Europe on Powell Street, designed in 1882 by J.E. Parr and T.A. Fee, who specialized in "the production of buildings that will pay... *Utilitas* is their motto, and revenue their aim," the Chinese Freemasons Building, a combined Italian/Chinese confection on West Pender Street, dating from 1901, and the handsome Art Deco Marine Building on Burrard Street, which was the tallest and finest building in the city during the early 1930s, are still proudly standing. Perhaps the favourite reminder of the town that Gassy Jack Deighton started is old Gastown itself. After its initial growth spurt, the original Gastown sank slowly into a skid row neighbourhood, as Vancouver's business activity moved to what Vancouverites call the Eastern Business District, an area embracing streets such as Granville,

Howe, Georgia, Pender, Hastings and Cordova.

Gastown began to enjoy a minor revival in the 1960s, as some of the old buildings were turned into restaurants and shops. Finally, in February 1971, the provincial government declared Gastown and most of nearby Chinatown historic areas. Gastown got a much needed facelift as a result. The once dilapidated buildings have been refurbished, and today antique shops, cafés, galleries, smart restaurants, pubs and fine stores fill the former warehouses and "two-bit" hotels of the old town.

The new look of Vancouver architecture is every bit as striking as the old. Perhaps the architect who has made the greatest impression on the city is Arthur Erickson. The Macmillan Bloedel Building on West Georgia Street, much of Simon Fraser University on Burnaby Mountain, and the Robson Square Law Court complex are all striking examples of Erickson's outstanding talent. Other dynamic sights of the new Vancouver include 60,000-seat B.C. Place Stadium, the world's largest (4 hectares, about 10 acres) air-supported dome stadium, the University of British Columbia's Museum of Anthropology (also an Erickson design), which is home to a stunning display of Indian art and artifacts including a spectacular grouping of totem poles; the Bloedell Conservatory, with its triodetic dome that commands a 360-degree view of the city and its environs, and the Harbour Centre complex on West

Below: a night view of the British Columbia Place Stadium and the lights of Vancouver. Facing page: the Vancouver Yacht Club.

Hastings Street. The revolving observation deck and restaurant perched at the top of the complex, reached by a dizzying glass skylift ride 180m up into the heavens, make the Harbour Centre one of the most visible landmarks on the Vancouver skyline.

But for that glimpse into tomorrow which forward-looking Vancouver always seems to typify, you need to visit Canada Place and Expo Centre, both part of Vancouver's great 1986 Centenary birthday present to itself and the world, EXPO '86.

EXPO '86's official theme, World in Motion – World in Touch, celebrates human achievement and aspirations in transportation and communication – on land, water, and in the air. All the provinces of Canada, more than 40 nations of the world, including Australia, Romania, Sri Lanka, Kenya, Pakistan, Japan, Yugoslavia, Barbados, Saudi Arabia, Costa Rica, the U.S.A., the U.S.S.R., the People's Republic of China (the first time the big three have been together on one site), the Republic of Korea, the Philippines, Hungary, Mexico and many, many more; some of British Columbia's neighbours across the

These pages: views of Vancouver, with its pleasing combination of modern architecture and a stunning natural setting.

border, and numerous internationally renowned corporations, joined with Vancouver and British Columbia to showcase this fascinating theme. Tall ships and space ships, hieroglyphics and lasers, bark boats and magnetic levitation trains, the treasures of the Mayans and robots of the twenty-first century – all were on display at this ingenious exposition of the world's technology. But EXPO '86 was more than just mind-boggling: thanks to the World Festival it was a cultural extravaganza of ballet and music and art and folk-lore and dance expressing the artistic diversity of all the world's peoples. And it was a taste sensation. Vancouver, with its cosmopolitan population, already boasts some of the best eating experiences in North America; adding the culinary delights of six continents for EXPO '86 just increased the city's love affair with food and fine dining.

A five-and-a-half month imagination extravaganza, EXPO '86 took place on two locations right in the heart of Vancouver: the north shore of False Creek and at the Canada Pavillion at Canada Place on Burrard Inlet. The combined site covered some 70 hectares (173 acres).

EXPO '86 provided such a stimulating feast for the senses that it's hard to pick favourite events or exhibits. Certainly some of the highpoints of the world exposition included the elegant Canada Pavillion, which with its five billowing sails looked very much like one of the giant ocean liners that opened up Vancouver to the world and international commercial status, and the 17-storey geodesic Expo Centre, home of the 500-seat OMNIMAX Theatre's amazing film "A Freedom to Move." The theatre's enormous, 27-metre screen showing images nine times larger than those of normal movie screens transported the viewer from the frozen tundra of the North Pole to the sun-baked flats of the Mojave Desert – and beyond to the farthest reaches of the world.

Then there was the spectacular

These pages: the magnificent, Victorian-style Parliament Buildings in Victoria, capital of British Columbia. Overleaf: the colourful Butchart Gardens, north of Victoria.

Highway 86, an undulating, four-lane freeway of steel and concrete rising 12m (39 feet) up from the waters of False Creek. This 217-metre-long (711 feet) fantasy highway of the future came complete with traffic jams, sailing regattas and a submarine poking up from an adjoining garden to check out the action. While Lamborghini and Maserati demonstrated the splendours of auto speed, Italian style, the Japanese undoubtedly stole the show with their HSST (High Speed Surface Transport) magnetic-levitation train. Capable of reaching 450kph, this transport marvel literally flies along the tracks – a centimetre above them – for the smoothest ride imaginable.

For all EXPO '86 was definitely a premier vacation-fun experience, it also provided future-watch experts and the public with the opportunity to observe and evaluate up-and-coming trends in specialized transportation areas such as Marine Commerce, Polar Transportation and Communication, Search and Rescue, Human-Powered Transportation and Communications and Mobility for Elderly and Disabled People.

Vancouver is well used to visitors, so the millions of extra guests who came to the city for EXPO '86 were assured of a hospitable welcome. Even without EXPO '86's many attractions, some of which, like the Canada Pavillion and Expo Centre, remain as permanent fixtures, this is a city made for sightseeing and good times. Shopping is excellent, especially along Robsonstrasse – as its name suggests, a gift to Vancouver from its European immigrants. Vancouver's Chinatown, the largest in North America after San Francisco, abounds with twisting streets of fine restaurants and shops filled with exotic merchandise from the Orient. (Chinese New Year – a riotous celebration of dragons, drums, parades, firecrackers, costumes and great food – is definitely a not-to-be-missed event.) Bordering on Vancouver's presti-ious Shaughnessy district is the South Granville shopping area, a mecca of art galleries, boutiques, exquisite jewels, stylish furs and top quality fashions.

While many people visit Vancouver – it is one of the major convention centres of North America – all too many of these visitors enjoy themselves so much here that their stay is over before they have a chance to see some of the bountiful province beyond this handsome city. This really is too bad.

Premier Bill Bennett said of B.C.'s Pavillion at EXPO '86, "... This is truly our show, our opportunity to set an indelible imprint on the world." Well, all of beautiful British Columbia, like Vancouver, is guaranteed to leave an indelible imprint on visitors lucky enough to experience all that this richly endowed province has to offer.

Below: the Empress Hotel, on Victoria's Inner Harbour (facing page). Overleaf: the Prince George sailing up the Inside Passage.